Vancouver

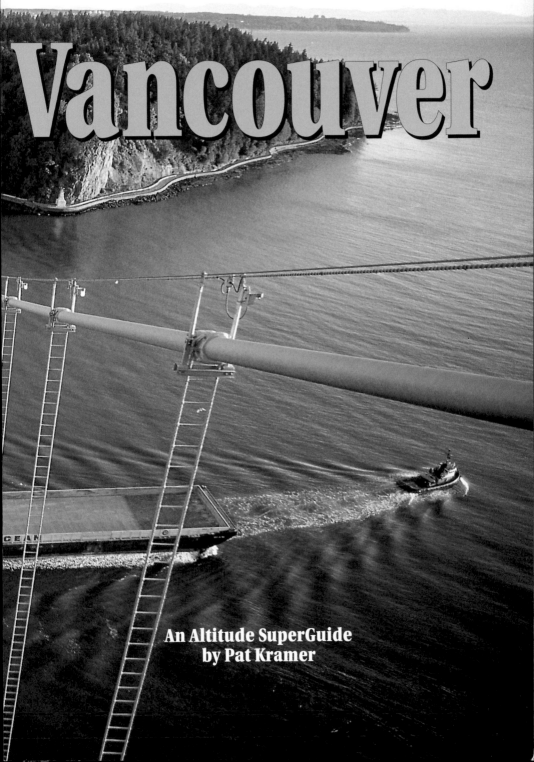

Vancouver

An Altitude SuperGuide
by Pat Kramer

Publication Information

Altitude Publishing Canada Ltd.
The Canadian Rockies / Vancouver
1500 Railway Avenue
Canmore, Alberta T1W 1P6
www.altitudepublishing.com
Copyright 1999, 2002 © Pat Kramer

Extreme care has been taken to ensure that all information presented in this book is accurate and up-to-date, and neither the author nor the publisher can be held responsible for any errors.

Canadian Cataloguing in Publication Data
Kramer, Pat
Vancouver
Includes index.
ISBN 1-55153-614-5
1. Vancouver (B.C.)--Guidebooks. I. Title.
FC3847.18.K72 1998   917.11'33044   C98-910750-7
F1089.5.V22K72 1998

Made in Western Canada

Printed and bound in Western Canada by Friesen Printers, Altona, Manitoba.

Altitude GreenTree Program

Altitude Publishing will plant in Western Canada twice as many trees as were used in the manufacturing of this product.

We acknowledge the financial support of the Government of Canada through the Book Publishing Industry Development Program (BPIDP) for our publishing activities.

Photographs
Front cover: Vancouver skyline at dusk
Inset left: Totem pole, detail
Inset right: Capilano Suspension Bridge
Frontispiece: Lion's Gate Bridge
Back cover: Canada Place

Project Development
Concept/art direction	Stephen Hutchings
Design/layout	Kelly Stauffer
Editor	Sabrina Grobler
Maps	Mark Higenbottam
Index	Elizabeth Bell
Financial management	Laurie Smith

A Note from the Publisher
The world described in *Altitude SuperGuides* is a unique and fascinating place. It is a world filled with surprise and discovery, beauty and enjoyment, questions and answers. It is a world of people, cities, landscape, animals and wilderness as seen through the eyes of those who live in, work with, and care for this world. The process of describing this world is also a means of defining ourselves.

It is also a world of relationship, where people derive their meaning from a deep and abiding contact with the land—as well as from each other. And it is this sense of relationship that guides all of us at Altitude to ensure that these places continue to survive and evolve in the decades ahead.

Altitude SuperGuides are books intended to be used, as much as read. Like the world they describe, *Altitude SuperGuides* are evolving, adapting and growing. Please write to us with your comments and observations, and we will do our best to incorporate your ideas into future editions of these books.

Stephen Hutchings

Stephen Hutchings
Publisher

Contents

Introduction

A Spectacular Setting. 7
Vancouver Neighbourhoods 11
Native Culture. 20
History 22
Vancouver's Environment 24

Features & Attractions

Downtown & West End 27
North Shore 31
Special Interest 32
Festivals 33
Trade Shows 34
Kids 36

Shopping & Strolling

Self-guided Half-day Driving Tours 43
Strolling Tours. 49
Shopping Areas. 58

Culture & Recreation

History of the Arts. 71
Galleries 72
Performing Arts. 75
Museums & Planetariums. 78
Literary Arts 80
Music 80
Pubs, Nightclubs & Late-night entertainment . . 82
Professional Sports. 89
Recreation
  Bicycling 91
  Running. 92
  Water Sports 94
  Golf. 96
  Snowboarding & Skiing 96
  Easy Walks & Hikes 98

Vancouver Restaurants. 105
Reference & Index 114

Maps

Vancouver Overview 8-9
Granville Island 55
Stanley Park. 60
Downtown. 64

The *Vancouver SuperGuide* is organized according to this colour scheme:

Introduction

Features & Attractions

Shopping & Strolling

Culture & Recreation

Restaurants

Reference & Index

A Spectacular Setting

Overlooking downtown Vancouver at dusk

Vancouver is a magical place. There are few other major cities on earth (and no others in Canada) where you can golf a challenging course in the morning, spend the afternoon sailing among sheltered isles, have an elegant dinner on a mountaintop, then indulge in a night skiing

adventure high above twinkling city lights.

Greater Vancouver is tucked into the southwest corner of Canada. The largest city in the province of British

Vancouver's Weather

Mean temperature	11 °C (52 °F)
High mean (June 30)	29 °C (84 °F)
Low mean (Jan. 8)	4.4 °C (40 °F)
Annual precipitation	94 cm (37 in.)
Number of days rain	136
Number of days snow	5
Number of days thunder	2
Number of days fog	17
Hours of sunshine	2,162

Source: Vancouver Weather Office

Columbia is located approximately 40 km north of the U.S. border and surrounded on three sides by water—Burrard Inlet to the north, the Strait of Georgia to the west, and the north arm of the Fraser River to the south. Most noticeable upon arrival is the remarkably serene setting. This contrasts with the highrises of downtown, a tightly packed district on a traffic-filled peninsula that features a forested "greenspace"—1,000 acre Stanley Park. Across the blue-gray ocean inlet, spanned by the suspension cables of the

Lion's Gate Bridge are the North Shore Mountains, part of the Coastal Range. These mountainsides are dotted with tungsten lights, which identify Grouse Mountain. The smaller patch of lights mark Seymour Mountain farther to the east. Just north of the scenic mountains are vast expanses of wilderness— dense forests and tundra spaces scattered all the way to the North Pole. Beyond Vancouver's undulating coastal mountains, there are bears, wildlife, forestry camps, provincial and national parks, lakes and seemingly endless

left: False Creek harbour

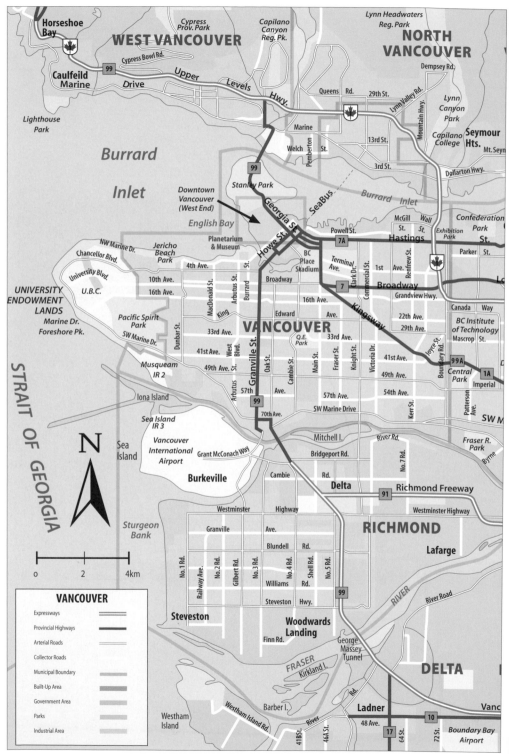

VANCOUVER

Expressways
Provincial Highways
Arterial Roads
Collector Roads
Municipal Boundary
Built-Up Area
Government Area
Parks
Industrial Area

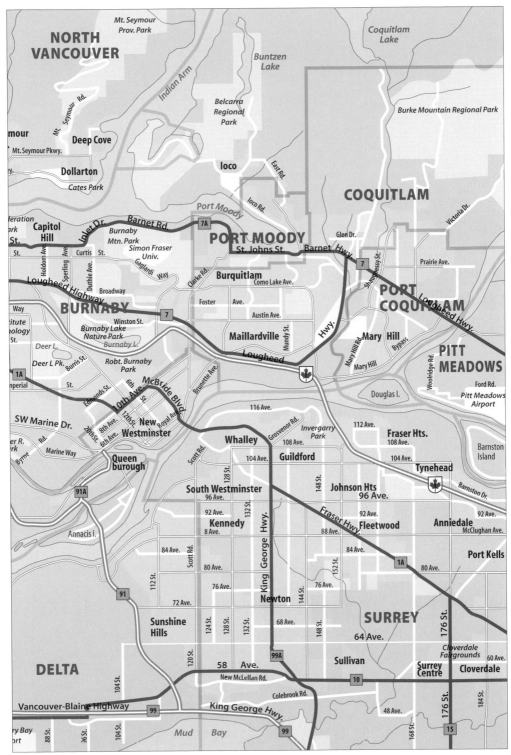

Summer at English Bay

chains of mountains. German visitors aptly call Vancouver "The city pushed up against the wilderness."

Vancouver is nearly the midpoint on the west coast of North America and is equidistant by air from London and Tokyo. While Vancouver's inner core has the second smallest area of eight major Canadian cities, it has a geographic surface area of 44 square miles. The total metropolitan area of sprawling "Greater" Vancouver with its surrounding municipalities is 1,076 square miles, making it the third largest metropolitan area in Canada.

This guide covers the best attractions and restaurants within the tight-knit city core of Vancouver and the scenic North Shore, including the municipalities of North Vancouver and West Vancouver immediately across the water from the downtown. These are the scenic areas a visitor will want to experience during a short, sweet visit.

Vancouver has a soggy reputation—it is often described as a sort of moistened sponge disguised as a city. Misty showers and cloudy skies are common; this is a fact. But rarely does it rain heavily and mercifully, mud is rare. Frequent rain showers keep Vancouver clean and green.

Admittedly, the local expression, " If you don't like the weather, wait a minute, it will change" is no exaggeration. Often, clouds roll in unexpectedly to interrupt the promise of blue skies. For the months

The Best City

Municipality or district	Claim to fame
Burnaby	Lake trails; parks
Delta and Langley	Verdant farmlands
Maple Ridge and Fort Langley	Hearty pioneer spirit
New Westminster	A fresh food market; maritime history
North Vancouver and West Vancouver	Mountain peaks and trails; sandy coves; waterfront parks
Port Coquitlam, Coquitlam and Port Moody	Mountain parks; logging history
Richmond	Asian shopping and restaurants; fishing boats, movie theatre complex
Surrey	Shopping; fast-growing urban area
Vancouver	Tourist attractions; parks; shopping
White Rock	Sandy beaches and sunsets

Gastown at night

of July through September, however, the average daytime high temperature is over 22 °C (75 °F), and there are usually enough sunny, hot days to keep visitors and residents alike in good spirits. From October through November, warm, lingering, relatively dry spells are the norm.

As for the rest of the year, while most of Canada is counting snowflakes, the warm Japanese ocean current allows Vancouverites to count tiny spring flower buds. All this mild weather leads to several local sayings including, "We keep the snow in the mountains where it belongs"; "I'd rather shovel rain anytime"; "It isn't raining, it's dripping liquid sunshine"; and the equally infamous local boast, "One day last January I went scuba diving in the morning and skiing in the afternoon."

The best way to fit into the Vancouver lifestyle is to forget the rain and get serious about quality leisure time. Vancouverites read more, shop more, eat out more, smoke less and take longer coffee breaks than anywhere else in North America. They also buy more sports equipment, own more boats, attend more fitness classes and ski more than people who live anywhere else in Canada. West Coast weather is at the heart of this lifestyle.

Vancouver Weather Updates are available by taped message at (604) 664-9032, (604) 664-9010 or (604) 299-9000, extension 3501.

Greater Vancouver: Its Cities and Neighbourhoods

Cities

The monolithic Greater Vancouver region, estimated to stretch over 1,076 square miles, is comprised of several surrounding districts and municipalities. Each has its own mayor and city council, and runs its own hospitals and school system.

A Great City?

In March 1995, the Corporate Resources group in Geneva, Switzerland released a ranking of 118 cities based on their living and environmental conditions. The City of Vancouver won a silver medal as the second best city in the world. Vancouver's City Administration ranked sixth for public service, efficiency and infrastructure. The top cities in this survey were: Singapore, Vancouver, Auckland, Wellington, Vienna and Dusseldorf. This places Vancouver first in North America.

In 1997, Santa Fe-based *Outside* magazine decided Vancouver was in the top ten of the "world's best hometowns" based on its parks and nearby wilderness areas. Its greatest drawbacks are usually listed as the high cost of housing and congested traffic. Add to that the frequent car break-ins and petty crime in the downtown area.

Population Count

Greater Vancouver's total population, 2002, is estimated to be about 2.0 million and rising rapidly. In the last decade, growth has averaged over 2 per cent per year.

Vancouver from the air

Vancouver's Neighbourhoods

East Side Neighbourhoods

Grandview-Woodlands is a hip older neighbourhood with a diverse social and ethnic makeup. Commercial Drive is the main drag that features assorted little shops, an occasional Italian flare, hints of an Asian presence and alternative-lifestyle stops.

Hastings-Sunrise/Renfrew-Collingwood is an older working-class neighbourhood undergoing significant development near the SkyTrain stations. Young families and couples are attracted here by the area's proximity to downtown.

Riley Park/Kensington-Cedar Cottage is an ethnically diverse neighbourhood with an eclectic mix of stores along Cambie, Main and Kingsway streets. There are also numerous parks, cafés and some

great views. There are choice antique shops along Main Street, plus the oft-visited Queen Elizabeth Park on 33rd Ave and Cambie, and nearby Nat Bailey Stadium, home of the triple-A Vancouver Canadians baseball team.

Strathcona/Mt. Pleasant, one of Vancouver's oldest neighbourhoods, is somewhat decrepit, though slow redevelopment is giving it Canada's largest concentration of artists' studio lofts à la New York. Its strong points are Chinatown's scarlet-coloured, shop-lined streets along Pender and Keefer streets and Dr. Sun Yat-Sen Classical Chinese Garden, 578 Carrall St., (604)689-7133. The area's less appealing features include: dilapidated rooming houses, soup kitchens and homeless shelters to the north, and industrial lands combined with low-rise condos to the south.

Sunset/Fraserview/Killarney is one of Vancouver's nicest modest neighbourhoods. Though shabby in some spots, it is close to downtown, and peaceful residential streets offer good views of the Fraser River delta. Its best features are "Little India" or the Punjabi Market south of 49th and Main, a southern Asian shopping and restaurant district, and the Fraserview Golf Course, 7800 Vivian Drive.

West Side Neighbourhoods

Arbutus Ridge/Kerrisdale is a leafy, affluent neighbourhood with tree-lined streets, well-reputed schools and some wonderful views of the North Shore. Its many seniors enjoy the relatively expensive shopping around 41st Ave. and Arbutus St., (604)732-4255.

Dunbar/Point Grey is another treed neighbourhood,

home to a diverse mix of university students, middle-income families and First Nations people. Bordered by English Bay to the north and the Fraser River to the south, the area has several large, sandy public beaches along Northwest Marine Drive, spectacular views and an array of green spaces. Its pros are the University of British Columbia (U.B.C.), (604) 822-2211, on the tip of Point Grey and Pacific Spirit Regional Park (604) 224-5739 , headquartered at 16th Ave. and Blanca St. This park features miles of hiking and mountain biking trails. The U.B.C . Museum of Anthropology, 6393 Northwest Marine Drive, (604) 822-3825, houses an impressive collection of First Nations artifacts.

Wreck Beach, accessible via a rugged trail, is an alternative-lifestyle, neo-hippie nudist beach.

Fairview/South Cambie is an energetic neighbourhood with heavy traffic, good shopping and a hip urban atmosphere. False Creek, a pedestrian-oriented residential community, has a friendly waterfront Seawall to explore, but

Vancouver's Best Crowd Scenes

Name	The scene and best timing	Location
Chinatown	With its exotic medicines, foreign languages and delectable Asian foods, this street is always a flurry of activity, especially on weekends.	West Pender and nearby Keefer St., Vancouver
First, Second and Third Beach, Stanley Park	On sunny summer days the concessions and change houses are busy and Second Beach's wading pool is filled to capacity. Third Beach is a showcase for what healthy living and exercise can do for a young, lithe body.	Start at the foot of Denman St., Vancouver at First Beach and continue to stroll
Festivals and special celebrations	At these times, Vancouver's locals—professional crowd minglers all—strut their stuff.	Various venues
Gastown	Echoing a certain bygone charm and offering a wide range of polite street vendors, a stop at a sidewalk café lets the whole world pass you by.	Start at The Landing, Gastown, 375 Water St., Vancouver
Granville Island and its Public Market	Here is the place where Vancouver seems to be in love with itself. No matter that the market vendors make exceptionally vast profits, it's all so wholesome that no one seems to mind.	Start at Granville Island Public Market, 1689 Johnstone St., Vancouver
Lonsdale Quay Market	Offering a bird's-eye view of downtown Vancouver, this is just the place to stretch out in the sun on the front deck almost any day and do some healthy munching and people-watching. Go upstairs. Taking the Sea Bus here is half the fun.	123 Carrie Cates Court, foot of Lonsdale, North Vancouver
Queen Elizabeth Park and Quarry Gardens	For the most unusual overlook anywhere, time your visit for a summer Saturday from 1 p.m. to 4 p.m. when brides by the dozen come to be photographed.	33rd and Cambie St., Vancouver
Robson Street or Robsonstrasse	Shopping, strolling and drinking coffee with lots of young company, this area buzzes every night, and is extra loud on Friday and Saturday nights in the summer.	Robson Street between Burrard and Bute
West Vancouver Centennial Seawall	Beside this always-active 2 km (1.2 mile) paved walk along the ocean, from late May through September between 5 p.m. and 7 p.m., cruise ships pass nearby. Then the sun sets.	Dundarave Pier in the 2400 block, Marine Drive, West Vancouver

the destination point is usually the heavily patronized Granville Island, Johnstone and Duranleau streets, (604) 666-5784, a waterfront public market featuring fresh produce, bistros, sidewalk entertainment, galleries and craft shops.

Kitsilano is a funky beach community with a so-called "California" ambiance, bikini-clad blondes and muscular beefcakes. Once home to a large population of hippies in late 1960s, today it caters more to yuppies and trendy twenty-somethings who enjoy the area's cafés, bookstores, boutiques and jazzy restaurants. Start by exploring the bustling area around Kitsilano Park at the north foot of Yew St., a sandy waterfront park with a pool. The H.R. MacMillan Planetarium, 1100 Chestnut St., (604) 738-STAR, related museums like the Vancouver Maritime Museum, 1905 Ogden Ave., (604)257-8300, and kite flying in Vanier Park are also popular attractions.

Oakridge/Marpole is a middle- and upper-middle-income neighbourhood experiencing a decade-long influx of Asian immigrants—many from Hong Kong. This has resulted in the construction of boxy so-called "monster homes." The neighbourhood is complemented by the Langara Golf Course, 6706 Alberta St., (604)257-8357 and Oakridge Shopping Centre, 650 West 41st, (604)261-2511.

Shaughnessy is Vancouver's oldest and most prestigious neighbourhood, now housing the staff of several international consulates. Its curving, tree-lined boulevards

Sea Bus

and heritage homes in English arts and craft, Tudor, Georgian or colonial revival styles are close to downtown Vancouver. Real estate prices range from $1 million for a simple fixer-upper to $12 million. Van-Dusen Botanical Garden, 5251 Oak St., (604)878-9274, once the area's golf course, is now a 52-acre public show garden.

West End/downtown, considered an exciting cosmopolitan neighbourhood with a substantial gay population, is most noted for its boutiques, restaurants, cafés and bookstores, pleasantly accessible by

Local Vocabulary

back east	The rest of Canada
chuck, saltchuck	The ocean or other large body of water
coho	Any great-tasting salmon; see "pink" in this table
cold wine & beer store	Legal private outlet
First Narrows	Local name for the "Lions Gate Bridge"
foot of …	Where the street terminates in the ocean or a river
"parking lots"	The freeways and sidestreets during rushhour(s)
pink	A pale, ordinary-tasting salmon
prawns	Very large, gourmet shrimp
quitting early	Leaving work at 1 p.m. or 2 p.m. or as soon as offices begin to close in the Eastern Standard Time zone (as early as noon on Fridays)
Sea Bus	A public transit foot ferry
SkyTrain	A public transit vehicle on an elevated track
stress puppy	Someone who does not know how to enjoy their leisure time
"the Island"	The city of Victoria
Washington	The state, not the eastern U.S. capital city

Asian cooks enjoy their own creations

pedestrian-filled side streets. There are some gritty, dangerous sections in the northeast. Among the office buildings is the notable district of Yaletown, on Hamilton and Mainland streets, a stylish retro-shopping district often used as a movie set location. The densely populated downtown is addressed at length in this guidebook, which features Stanley Park, English Bay, historic Gastown, superb shopping, excellent restaurants and the most beautiful views. Its greatest disadvantages are limited parking, heavy traffic, dense populations, increasing petty theft and car break-ins.

Ethnic Neighbourhoods

A visit to any of these communities offers new perspectives and a chance to touch the multicultural face of Vancouver. Over 60 multicultural groups exert their influence on the Vancouver mosaic. For recorded information, phone (604) 299-9000. For information about multicultural festivals and events, dial extension 3234.

Cantonese restaurants and the flavours of the north, including garlic-laced Mandarin (Peking) cuisine and spicy Szechuan dishes, are found along this street. Butcher shops sell barbecued pork, chicken and duck in forms unfamiliar to regular supermarket shoppers, and you will see rows of lok chur—Chinese sausages hung with red strings. Fish are sold whole and very fresh, and those looking for gifts will find calligraphy brushes, porcelain ornaments, vases, knickknacks and some jewelry. Herbalists will prepare a bundled remedy for conditions such as fatigue. Dr. Sun Yat-Sen Classical Chinese Garden on 578 Carrall St, (604) 689-7133, offers ongoing guided tours that explain the recurring theme of yin and yang.

Greektown is a small area of assorted shops around the intersection of MacDonald and Broadway. Food stores with large selections of olives, feta cheeses and tiny melitzanes, fish, bread and sweets outlets, and several record stores selling bouzouki music can be found here. St. George's Orthodox Cathedral, 4500 Arbutus St., invites visitors to its incense-filled services, (604) 266-7148. Greek restaurants are scattered here and throughout Vancouver.

Although there are Japanese restaurants located throughout Vancouver, the

Best Bets: Vancouver From the Water

Take the MV *Constitution,* a paddlewheeler offering daily tours or dinner cruises from the north foot of Denman Street near the Bayshore Hotel. For reservations, call Vancouver Harbour Cruises, (604) 688-7246.

Private boats and yachts of all shapes and sizes offer cruises and water mini-adventures from the marina behind Bridges (Restaurant), Granville Island, west waterfront. Look for the yellow roof. Contact Vancouver Tourism, (604) 683-2000 and ask for the current charter boat listings or call the Granville Island Information Centre, (604)666-5784. A charter is not as expensive as you may think.

Take the public transit Sea Bus. For a 12-minute one-way crossing from downtown to Lonsdale Quay, a fresh food market on the North Shore, board the "floating" bus that makes its way across the inlet. Turn up at Waterfront Station, 200 Burrard St., or ask for advice from Public Transit Customer Information, (604) 521-0400; or (604) 299-9000, extension 2233.

heart of old Japantown is a diminutive area consisting mostly of grocery stores, which are concentrated around Oppenheimer Park between Dunlevy and Jackson streets (facing onto the 300 and 400 block on Powell St.). An ethnic festival is held in August. The old town was severely disrupted by a forced relocation program in 1942, but the flood of Japanese tourists into Vancouver since the 1980s has resulted in numerous Japanese-owned shops catering specifically to Japanese tourist needs on all Vancouver's major shopping streets. Nitobe Memorial Garden, near the Museum of Anthropology, 6393 NW Marine Drive, (604) 822-6038, is an authentic and serene Japanese garden.

The East Side's Grandview-Woodlands is the community of choice for those with bohemian inclinations. Poets, artists and various eccentric wannabes mix with Asian shopkeepers and Italian restaurateurs. The area's main drag along Commercial Drive (from the 1000 block to the 2000 block or between Hastings and 1st Ave.) is simply dubbed "Little Italy." Countless interesting coffee houses, old-style trattorias, grocery stores, pasta outlets, alternative bookstores, ethnic restaurants and cool clothing boutiques add to the area's charm. Plan to shop for shoes. The breads and sweets are authentically Italian, as are the cheeses, veal and homemade sausages.

The Punjabi Market or "Little India" stretches for about three blocks along Main St. and 49th Ave., and is a southern Asian shopping and restaurant district. Spice shops, 18 places to buy East Indian jewelry and 25 fabric stores are the gems of this area. Its sweet shops are legendary and the food stores are filled with the pungent aromas of items from ghee to jackfruit and Bombay duck. Farther afield is the Ross Street Temple at Marine Drive and Ross Street. Its award-winning design was created for the Sikh community by legendary architect Arthur Erickson. It is one of more than 15 Sikh temples in Vancouver. Restaurants featuring typical dishes from the Indian sub-continent are scattered here and throughout Vancouver.

Shipping

Annually, the Port of Vancouver is visited by more than 3,000 foreign vessels and handles more than 70 million metric tonnes of cargo. (A tonne or "metric ton" is 2,204 pounds, slightly larger than a 2,000-pound ton.) The second busiest port in the world in terms of tonnage (New York is first), Vancouver is the largest exporter in the world for grain and wood products. The Port of Vancouver facilitates trade with over 90 nations with its prime customers in the far East: Japan, the Soviet Union and China. Generating almost 11,000 jobs, the Port contributes $1 billion each year to Vancouver's economy.

There are four key shipping sectors: bulk, general cargo,

Vancouver Visitor Helplines

Drop into the main Vancouver Tourist facility for loads of brochures, maps, directions and advice. Vancouver Tourism is located at Plaza Level, Waterfront Centre, 200 Burrard St., Vancouver right across from Canada Place "Under the Sails." Other travel information centres are located throughout the city.

North Shore Tourism will help visitors answer questions about the North Shore (604) 987-4488.

Vancouver, Coast and Mountain Tourism will help visitors answer questions about the Lower Mainland, (604)739-9011; 800-667-3306

SuperNatural British Columbia Reservation and Information Service provides publications, accommodations, recommendations, ski advice, camping and general how-to for all areas of the province. Contact (800) 663-6000 or within Vancouver, (604) 663-6000.

BC Public Transit Customer Information provides personalized assistance with schedules and routes, (604) 521-0400; or (604) 299-9000, extension 2233.

BC Public Transit routes are mapped out and described in the BC Yellow Pages on pages 33 to 36.

A public transit booklet describing all transit routes is available free or for $1 at all travel information centres, public libraries and chambers of commerce.

Car rentals are in the BC TEL Yellow Pages under "Automobile Renting."

Floating homes in False Creek

container and the cruise ship industry. Huge shipping terminals dot the waterfront. All operate under federal (not provincial) jurisdiction.

In the bulk category, 23 different grades of grain are stored in the mammoth cement cylinders at Pacific Elevators, Alberta Pool, Saskatchewan Wheat Pool, Pioneer Grain Terminals and United Grain Growers Ltd. In a crop season, each terminal moves an average of two to three million tonnes including wheat, barley, canola, rye and grain by-products. Westshore Terminals at Roberts Banks, one of the largest coal-handling facilities in the world, ships more than 20 million tonnes of bulk coal each year.

Vancouver ports are responsible for components that make up much of the world's agricultural fertilizers—sulphur, phosphate and potash.

Vancouver Wharves ships mineral concentrates, dry fertilizers, methanol, pulp and paper, potash from Saskatchewan and sulphur—a byproduct of Alberta's very sour gas. Dry bulk sulphur is brilliant yellow and has no smell. Potash is not gray, it looks like brown, dry dog food bits. Neptune Bulk Terminals in North Vancouver ships coal, potash, feed pellets, chemical fertilizers, canola oil and phosphate rock.

Pacific Coast Terminals Co. Ltd., CXY Chemicals Canada Ltd. and Dow Chemical Canada all ship dangerous and not-so-dangerous sulphur, ethylene glycol, styrene monomer, ethylene dichloride, muriatic acid and caustic soda solutions. Fibreco Export Ltd. ships out wood chips and lumber and BC Sugar imports about 140 billion tonnes a year.

Additionally, there are huge cranes in the Port of Vancouver to handle box containers. In June of 1997, the Deltaport container terminal doubled Vancouver's lucrative container-handling capacity. A single box container full of Gucci watches, for example, is worth far more in dollar value than many tonnes of bulk commodities.

The cruise industry accounts for around 120 cruise ship visits during the May to October season. Most of the 600,000 passengers who pass through Vancouver are headed for scenic Alaska. The Vancouver to Alaska cruise, with about 25 vessels, is the world's third most popular, after the Carribbean and the Mediterranean cruises.

A Portside Lifestyle

World-travelling pundits have noticed that busy seaports

Autumn in Stanley Park

seem to have different "personalities" from typical inland cities. Namely, there is a streak of something creative about them. Examples include Shanghai, New York, Marseilles and Liverpool. Shanghai, in contrast to other Chinese cities, is liberal and outward looking; New York belies the "friendliness" of America and its arts are legendary. Marseilles was the unruly seat of the French Revolution and Liverpool produced the Beatles and street fashions. The word "cosmopolitan" comes up in discussions of these places—something to do with the barrage of international influences that seaports constantly absorb. In this way, Vancouver is typical. Like other busy seaports of the world, Vancouver seems to have a certain open *joie de vivre* and a wild creative streak. In many ways it is not a typically Canadian city.

How is it different? Studies show that Vancouverites are more self-assured, fun-loving and devoted to leisure activities, read more books, spend more time shopping, and are less keen on special status for Quebec than anywhere else in Canada. Despite congested roadways and poor signage, they rage against building more roads, and routinely shift from pole to pole in politics. Enjoying better restaurant cuisine, drinking both more tea and coffee, supporting more public gardens, buying more sports equipment and taking longer coffee breaks than anywhere else in Canada, they are also North America's most resistant consumers. If a product or service sells here (an exceptionally great challenge), it will almost anywhere.

Of course, Vancouver has its typically Canadian aspects as well. Vancouverites are taxpaying, law-abiding, clean, friendly, tolerant people who defend Medicare, motherhood and moderation of public consumption, especially with regard to smoking, liquor and gambling. They tolerate a high degree of ethnic diversity and lifestyle choices. Like most Canadians, they resist rewarding outstanding performance or designating other Canadians as "heroes" or "stars" (with the exception of sports) and generally dislike shows of wealth. This Canadian trait is referred to by outsiders as "mediocrity" or "the bronze medal is good enough" mentality. Prime West Coast impulses are to protect the wilderness and its creatures, to set aside protected parks, and to support a united Canada.

The easiest way to feel at

ease in Vancouver is to be self-assured, respect nature, keep the city clean, plan out your leisure time, have some serious fun, be tolerant, eat healthy food and enjoy life over a cup of specialty coffee.

Hollywood North

With over 10,000 people employed in the tech-media work force, film and TV post-production, computer animation and video compression, and advanced film production, Vancouver is justly called "Hollywood North." Ranking just after Los Angeles (and far ahead of Toronto) as a busy movie and television venue,

BC recently edged out New York for second place in producing hour-long television dramas. During 1997, more than 80 productions took advantage of BC's spectacular physical settings including 18 feature films, 16 television series, 5 animation productions and 41 movies of the week.

"This land is your land," touts the glossy BC Film Commission brochure designed to attract American film producers. "We can give it to you for a song." Big players in the film industry use several studios (all off-limits to the public) for indoor shoots, but they frequently produce outdoor

scenes in Gastown, Chinatown or in Vancouver's back alleys. Long lines of parked white trailers are a good clue that a shoot is in progress—so is a police car marked "Seattle Police." Recent made-for-TV or feature movies have starred such actors as Morgan Fairchild, Lindsay Wagner, Terri Garr, Elizabeth Perkins, Goldie Hawn, Leslie Nielsen, Daniel Stern, Rob Lowe and Antonio Banderas. Recent feature film shoots have included *Deep Rising* and *Mr. Magoo* for Disney and *Firestorm* for Fox. In 1997, the largest budget film ever shot in British Columbia, the $100 million Disney feature film *Eaters of the Dead*, employed 900 people. Annually, an average of 44 television movies and feature films generate about $1 billion in spinoffs each year.

Ongoing TV series filmed here are many and include the popular X-Files and Millennium for Fox, Breaker High for United Paramount, and The Outer Limits and Stargate for MGM. In 1997, one local production firm, Rainmaker Inc., worked on 11 TV series.

The animation sector is also gaining popularity, producing digital effects for film, television and music videos. Vancouver companies create and produce the television cartoon series Reboot and Transformers for Mainframe Entertainment as well as Nilus the Sandman.

Watch for movie and television stars in downtown restaurants, pubs and in popular shopping areas. To catch the atmosphere, comb the listings on pages 119. No guarantees, but it is fun to try.

Performing Stars from Vancouver

Born in Vancouver in 1922 as Peggy Middleton, she embarked on a movie acting career but left her indelible slender black image on black-and-white television's The Munsters. Her name: Yvonne De Carlo.

This popular actress was born in Yellowknife, but grew up in Vancouver. She gained fame as swooning newspaperwoman Lois Lane in the movie *Superman* with Christopher Reeve. Her name: Margot Kidder.

This performer grew up in New Westminster, a suburb of Vancouver, and is now buried here. He was well known as the portly lawyer who never, ever lost a case, Perry Mason. His name: Raymond Burr.

This actor expected to be a bit player in Hollywood when he left his Burnaby home, but starring as materialistic Alex Keaton in television's Family Ties, he went on to make splashes in numerous movies including the

Back to the Future trilogy. His name: Michael J. Fox.

Many, many aspiring Vancouver actors have landed roles in TV's primetime but this hunk sets the likes of Tori Spelling and Tiffani-Amber Thiessen aflutter in Beverly Hills 90210. His name: Jason Priestly.

Well known for the theme song from the movie *Robin Hood* and many other soft rock hits, this avowed vegetarian now lives in London, England. His name: Bryan Adams.

Other performing artists from Vancouver include Jim Byrnes, Colin James, kd Lang, Long John Baldry, Tommy Chong, Rae Dawn Chong, Sarah McLachlan and jazz great, Dee Daniels.

In the "watch for him" category, this British singer/drummer comes to town to visit his son. His first ex-wife and her new husband live here. His name: Phil Collins.

Best Bets: Native Sites and Restaurants

Híwus Feast House Grouse Mountain—The Peak of Vancouver, 6400 Nancy Greene Way, North Vancouver, (604)984-0661, is a native-owned restaurant located on the top of Grouse Mountain. After a short guided journey through the forest to a sumptuous native-style feast adapted deliciously to modern tastes, costumed dancers and a drummer present authentic West Coast native dances. A panoramic Skyride or aerial tram takes visitors to this exciting mountaintop cultural eating experience. Reservations are recommended. Wheelchair accessible.

Liliget Feast House 1724 Davie St., (604)681-7044, run by Gitksan native Dolly Watts and her family, features tasty West Coast appetizers, main courses such as barbecued salmon or caribou, and desserts including tart soapberry ice cream and favourites adapted from traditional West

Totems

Coast native cooking. Reservations are recommended.

The Totem Pole Collection, at the foot of Geor-

gia Street (follow Park Road to Stanley Park), was first assembled in the 1920s. An estimated 10 million visitors pass

Vancouver's First Nations Festivals

Aboriginal Cultural Festival draws more than 20,000 people to a spectacle of native entertainers, arts and crafts, carvers and tasty fast food. Held in August, information is available from the Aboriginal Friendship Centre, 1607 East Hastings, Vancouver, (604) 251-4844.

Capilano Suspension Bridge Totem Pole Raising is an annual affair usually held on Mother's Day in May. Tsimshian carvers work all year on the

authentic totem pole raised at this event. Call in advance to confirm. Free parking, 10 minutes from downtown Vancouver. The facility is located at 3735 Capilano Road, North Vancouver or call (604) 985-7474.

Squamish Nation Canoe Races, a day of paddling, races, craft stalls and fast food is held in North Vancouver in July. For this year's time and location, call the North Shore travel information centre, (604) 987-4488.

Squamish Nation Powwow, a

day of prairie powwow dancing, dance competitions, singing, craft and food stalls is held in North Vancouver in July. For time and location, call the North Shore Travel information centre, (604)987-4488.

Whey-Ah-Wichen Canoe Races & Festival is an exciting day of war canoe races, craft stalls and barbecued salmon feasts held in North Vancouver in May. For timing and location, call the North Shore Travel information centre, (604) 987-4488.

by each year, making it the most viewed totem pole collection in the world. The painted poles are Kwakiutl; the unpainted pole is Gitksan. For a complete description, see the book entitled *Totem Poles* by Pat Kramer; it is sold on site.

U.B.C. Museum of Anthropology, 6393 NW Marine Drive, (604) 299-9000, extension 3825 or (604) 822-3825, has an excellent collection of ancient totem poles plus a wide assortment of masks, old engraved silver jewelry, black argillite pieces and carved wooden figures. Its centrepiece is Haida Bill Reid's sculpture, *The Raven and the First Men.*

Native Cuisine Adapted to Modern Tastes

- Bannock bread
- Buffalo burgers
- Smoked or barbecued salmon
- "Indian candy" or dried salmon
- Steamed clams or clam fritters
- Barbecued oysters
- Pan-fried oolichans
- Sweet potato with hazelnuts
- Barbecued caribou
- Chilled raspberry soup
- Roast venison
- Barbecued duck
- Smoked black Alaska cod
- Dried seaweed snacks
- Wildman salad
- Moose stew
- Steamed dulse seaweed

BC Native Arts

In general, most of the native arts sold in Vancouver are made by First Nations people. By purchasing their arts, you help to support both the artist and in many cases, his or her community.

BC Native Arts

Blue Raven Co., Suite 308 2545 West Broadway, Vancouver, (604) 224-1780

Cedar Root 1607 Hastings St. E., Vancouver, (604) 251-6244

Chocolate Arts, 2037 West 4th, Vancouver, (604) 739-0475

Coastal Peoples Fine Arts Gallery, Yaletown, 1072 Mainland Street, Vancouver; (604) 685-9298

Douglas Reynolds Gallery, South Granville, 2335 Granville Street, Vancouver; (604) 731-9292

Foster Walker Corporate Gifts and Baskets, 201,1200 West Pender Street, Vancouver, 800-668-8813, (604) 681-2456

Geomania, 1055 West Georgia, Vancouver, (604) 683-2818

Jade World, 1311 Howe St., Vancouver, (604) 733-7212

Lonsdale Quay Native Arts, 123 Carrie Cates Crescent, North Vancouver, (604) 990-9078

Spirit Wrestler Gallery, 8 Water Street, Vancouver, (604) 669-8813

The Anthropology Shop, 6393 NW Marine Drive, Vancouver, (604) 822-3825 or 299-9000 ext. 3825

The Raven and the Bear, 1528 Duranleau Street, Vancouver, (604) 669-3990

Vancouver Museum Shop, 1100 Chestnut Street, Vancouver, (604) 736-4431

Vancouver Art Gallery Shop, 750 Hornby Street, Vancouver, (604) 662-4700 or (604) 299-9000 ext. 5621

Wickaninnish Gallery, 1666 Johnston St., Vancouver, (604) 681-1057

Coast Salish Arts, 3917 West 51st Avenue, Vancouver, (604) 266-7374

Heritage Canada, 356 Water Street, Vancouver, (604) 669-6375

Hills Indian Crafts, Gastown, 165 Water Street, Vancouver, (604) 685-4249

Images for a Canadian Hgeritage, 164 Water Street, Vancouver, (604) 685-7046

Inuit Gallery, Gastown, 345 Water Street, Vancouver, (604) 688-7323

Khot-La-Cha Handicrafts, 270 Whonoak Street, North Vancouver, (604) 987-3339

Musuem of Anthropology Gift Shop, 6393 NW Marine Drive, Vancouver, (604) 822-3825 or 299-9000 ext. 3825

Silver Blue Traders Ltd., 1767 3rd Ave. W., Vancouver, (604) 737-1444

Vancouver Museum Gift Shop, 1100 Chestnut Street, Vancouver, (604) 736-4431

Wickaninnish Gallery, 1666 Johnstone Street, Vancouver, (604) 681-1057

Frog & The Lady Bud Native Arts, 456 Cordova St. W., Vancouver, (604) 687-4412

Gifts of the Raven, Vancouver International Airport, Richmond, (604) 303-3835

Eagle Spirit Gallery, 1803 Maritime Mews, Vancouver, (604) 801-5205

Marion Scott Gallery, 481 Howe St., Vancouver, (604)685-1934

Vancouver History

Centuries before western explorers discovered the lures of the Greater Vancouver area, this region was home to many aboriginal bands. These people traded with Captain Vancouver and the European and American pioneers who followed. Throughout the region, giant totem poles, centuries-old burial trees, tribal celebrations such as the "potlatch" continue to fascinate all those who pass this way.

More than 60 additional cultures have since migrated here and they too continue to leave their mark on the area. The legacy of early British settlers lives on, manifesting itself in trolley and double-decker bus tours and cosy English pubs. The Asian cultures thrive; North America's second largest Chinatown comes alive with street festivals, and there are Japanese karaoke and sushi bars galore. Vancouver's Italian district features a taste of the old country with delightful restaurants and specialty shops.

500 BC Coast Salish-speaking natives live in present-day Stanley Park in the summer.

1740s Russian sea otter pelt traders ply the West Coast interacting with the natives. Moscow stops sending traders supplies and they leave the area.

1791 Spanish Captain José Maria Navarez, in search of the Northwest Passage, anchors at Point Grey near the present-day University of British Columbia.

1792 Captain George Vancouver and his crew are warmly greeted by the Musquem band and enter Burrard Inlet.

1808 Explorer Simon Fraser completes a gruelling 35-day journey from Prince George to the ocean along Fraser's River.

1827 The Hudson's Bay Co. (HBC) founds Fort Langley outside Vancouver. In 1840 they establish Fort Victoria on Vancouver Island.

1846 The Oregon Treaty defines the 49th parallel as the division between the United States and the northern British Colony. Vancouver Island is allowed to dip below the 49th parallel; tiny San Juan Island is divided in half.

1850s Gold lures thousands of men, American and British, to Fraser's River and in 1863, to a rich inland strike at Barkerville. Colony Governor James Douglas frantically improvises roads, transportation services, taxation policies, law and order as American adventurers arrive unabated. Among the influx are Chinese who helped build U.S. railways.

1859 An American shoots a HBC trader's pig on San Juan Island; the ensuing Pig War leads to grave threats of U.S. naval invasion against sparsely populated New Caledonia (the early name for the British Columbia mainland). Later, San Juan becomes U.S. territory.

1862 The McCleery family, later billed "The Three Greenhorns," become Vancouver's first investing white settlers. Due to the potential for American naval invasion and the absence of British will to defend the territory, the Stanley Park area is designated a military reserve.

1863 Except for native people, the region's population is 90 per cent American. Prospectors and others send a petition to President Lincoln to annex the gold-laden region into the United States. Embroiled in a Civil War, eastern U.S. politicians ignore the request.

1867 Eastern Canada is united into a new dominion called "Canada" and the western Colony is immediately invited to join. Mr. "Gassy" Jack Deighton builds a saloon in Gastown. Tax collectors from Victoria arrive within months to remove his profits.

1871 British Columbia joins Canada with the promise to build a transcontinental railway. Queen Victoria personally names the new province.

1886 "Gastown" or Granville, population 1,000, is officially incorporated as the City of Vancouver. The first city council recommends that Stanley Park be preserved. On June 13, the Great Fire destroys most of the city's 600 wooden buildings; 21 people die. The Chinese construct shacks near Gastown; the area is notorious for opium and prostitution.

1887 Engine 374, pulling the first transcontinental passenger train for the Canadian Pacific Railway (CPR) arrives in Vancouver. The CPR builds the first Hotel Vancouver. Anti-Asiastic riots are severe. The Vancouver Electric Illuminating Co. lights up the streets.

1889 Lord Stanley, Governor General of Canada, dedicates Stanley Park to the people. Completion of the Vancouver Waterworks Dam gives residents running water.

1890 Vancouver's first streetcar service carries passengers for a nickel.

Vancouver History

1891 Actress Sarah Bernhardt performs at the new Opera House.

1892 The first paved street is Hastings and a golf course opens at Jericho. The economy falters as the U.S. goes into a major Depression.

1895 Soon-to-be-famous poetess Pauline Johnston, a Mohawk native, publishes her first book.

1897 On a boat returning from the Yukon, the bullet-riddled corpse of criminal "Soapy Smith" is accidentally switched with the body of former Vancouver mayor, Mr. Fred Cope. Vancouver citizens unknowingly bury the notorious outlaw in a civic funeral.

1898 Progress arrives in the form of a new railway station, a major newspaper and a movie theatre. George MacKay builds a hemp suspension bridge across Capilano Canyon on the forested North Shore. It becomes Vancouver's earliest tourist attraction.

1901 Tycoon B.T. Rogers founds BC Sugar and U.S. industrialist Andrew Carnegie donates money for a Carnegie Library.

1906 Chief Joe Capilano leads a native party to London to present his cause for native rights to King Edward VII, the "Great White Chief."

1907 Racial tensions explode and an angry mob descends on Chinatown. Later, the federal government gives $100,000 in compensation to the Chinese Benevolent Society.

1909 During the test run of Vancouver's first ambulance, the vehicle strikes and kills a tourist from Texas.

1914 326 East Indian refugees arriving on the Komogata Maru are detained, then sent away at gunpoint. Canada declares war; naval guns guard Stanley Park; men enlist.

1916 Prohibition closes saloons. In 1921 The Moderation Bill ends prohibition and many fortunes are founded through rum-running to the Americans during their ensuing prohibition period.

1918 The Spanish Flu claims 400 victims; World War I ends. Veterans return to massive unemployment. An earthquake shakes the city. 10,000 workers unite in a general strike.

1925 The first Second Narrows Bridge augments ferry services to the North Shore.

1929 Visiting escape artist Harry Houdini wows crowds. Boeing opens an aircraft factory in Coal Harbour and Victoria. Within weeks of Vancouver's Stock Exchange crash, the streets crawl with unemployed men.

1932 15 per cent of the population is on Relief; teachers work a month without pay.

1937 The Irish Guinness family finances the Lions Gate Bridge to service their new British Properties on Hollyburn Mountain, creating much-needed work. In

1939, King George and Queen Elizabeth officially open the bridge. Queen Elizabeth Park is established.

1941 Anti-aircraft guns are positioned in Stanley Park; women move into traditionally male jobs. A blackout is imposed on the city; residents fear an attack from Japan.

1942 Japanese residents are forcibly ordered into internment camps in the BC Interior.

1949 The first chairlift is built on Grouse Mountain.

1951 Princess Elizabeth and Prince Philip visit.

1953 CBC opens Vancouver's first television station.

1954 In the new sports stadium, Roger Bannister and John Landy both break four-minutes in the "Miracle Mile" at the British Empire Games.

1957 Elvis Presley performs at Empire Stadium.

1958 Nineteen construction workers die when the Second Narrows Bridge collapses.

1962 The TransCanada Highway forges a new link across Canada.

1970 The NHL's Vancouver Canucks play their first game.

1971 The Greenpeace environmental movement is founded in Vancouver. The West End is the most densely populated square mile in Canada. The Sea Bus begins operation. Chinatown is declared a historic area.

1972 Eccentric billionaire Howard Hughes and his entourage occupy the Bayshore Inn for four months.

1979 Granville Public Market opens on a former industrial zone.

1986 Tourism soars in the years after Vancouver hosts Expo '86, a successful World's Fair.

1993 Vancouver hosts a Summit Conference with U.S. President Bill Clinton and Russian President Boris Yeltsin.

1997 Vancouver hosts Asian leaders at an APEC conference.

1998 In the race to replace the internal combustion engine, Vancouver's Ballard Industries attract major investment from Ford Motor Company and Daimler-Benz.

Vancouver's Environment

In 1792, Captain George Vancouver and his crew were among the first Europeans to glimpse this rugged, forested area with its rolling mountains high above the ocean. He wrote in his ship's log that once settled, it would be "the most lovely country imagined." In 1935, Queen Elizabeth the Queen Mother was awestruck by her two days in Vancouver. In a rare moment of candor she exclaimed, "This must be the place to be." Over two hundred years later, British explorer Captain Vancouver's words were echoed during the 1993 World Summit. U.S. President Bill Clinton, while visiting with Premier Boris Yeltsin confided, "The beauty of Vancouver has inspired our work here."

Vancouver is home to some of the most breathtaking scenery in the world. Towering, snow-capped mountains rise high above a city adorned with ancient forests rolling in evergreen splendour toward the sparkling blue Pacific. Spreading inland from the coast is a sophisticated, cosmopolitan city that is struggling to seek harmony with the land.

Home to an enormous coastal temperate rainforest, multitudes of plant species and wildlife and an abundance of natural resources, the Vancouver Forest Region alone encompasses 13.7 million ha (34 million acres). It is home to eight different bio-climatic zones, two forested zones of coastal Douglas fir, western red cedar, Sitka spruce, western hemlock and red alder, rare or protected wildlife

including kermode bears, grizzly bears, marbled murrelets, killer whales and sea otters. In large measure, most of the population of British Columbia is directly or indirectly dependent on the province's natural resources for their livelihood and well-being. In addition to these pragmatic pressures, the region hosts enthusiastic visitors from North America, Asia and Europe for steelhead and salmon fishing, pleasure boating, wildlife viewing, mountain climbing, kayaking, hunting and camping.

Protecting the environment, the forest and water resources is fraught with complicated issues and conflicting interests. Governments, First Nations, industry workers, environmentalists and various stakeholders engage in discussions, study sessions, seminars, action committees and commissions. Through an ongoing land and resource management planning process, as well as the creation of a Lower Mainland Nature Legacy, protected areas around Vancouver now cover approximately 14 per cent of the Lower Mainland region, or 580,000 ha (1.4 million acres). Since 1992, the provincial government has also committed itself to preserving 12 per cent of the total provincial land base through the creation of 200 new provincial parks and protected areas.

By 1997, all forest companies were said to be in full compliance with the newly enacted British Columbia Forest Practices Code. The code, considered the most environmentally sensitive and comprehensive legislation

of its kind in the world, tightened the existing legislation. Can a complying BC forest company remain economically competitive against other regions of the world? This remains to be seen; the conflicts continue.

BC is host to almost every major world environmental association. Greenpeace, for example, originated in Vancouver in the 1960s. In 1997, Forests Minister David Zirnhelt and Environment, Lands and Parks Minister Cathy McGregor asked Greenpeace to abandon its activity on the Central Coast in favour of supporting First Nations, communities and other stakeholders who are seeking community-based land-use solutions. Greenpeace had been organizing action on logging levels and the protection of bear habitat.

One of the most visible environmental issues for Vancouver residents is that of watershed logging. In order to supply drinking water to 1.9 million Greater Vancouver residents, the forests visible on the upper North Shore Mountains and those in surrounding areas are "protected." However, timber interests continually pressure the Greater Vancouver Regional District (GVRD) to approve "limited" logging in the watersheds. Though diseased timber is prone to forest fires and needs to be culled, increased sedimentation from logging jeopardizes the purity of the supply. *Giardia lamblia*, a waterborne parasite also known as "beaver fever," has symptoms ranging from serious weight loss, acute diarrhea, stomach pains,

Vancouver's Environment

weakness, nausea and fever. Pristine watersheds are rarely implicated in outbreaks, so it is likely that humans, not wildlife, are responsible for its introduction into protected areas. When water is turbid (containing sediment), chlorine may not kill the disease. Industrial activities in watersheds, such as road building and logging, increase turbidity and the chances that *Giardia* will be introduced. Because of this risk to human health, the B.C. Medical Association (BCMA) opposes logging in watersheds.

Preservation of wildlife is an ever-urgent issue. BC's population of spotted owls, estimated to be about 100 pairs, or about four per cent of the total northern spotted owl population, are now permanently protected in forested areas more than 100 years old. Forest Renewal BC recently invested about $1 million in the Lower Mainland in conservation efforts and set aside a staggering 159,000 ha (393,000 acres) of major existing parks, as well as 18 special resource management zones totaling 204,000 ha (504,000 acres).

There are an estimated 20,000 grizzly bears in remote areas of British Columbia. The provincial grizzly bear conservation strategy, introduced in 1995, protects important grizzly habitat by creating protected areas such as the huge Khutzeymateen and Kitlope valleys. In addition, under the Forest Practices Code, wildlife habitats, including that of black bears and salmon, are carefully managed.

The need for accurate data remains imperative. For example, the B.C. Conservation Data Centre is a cooperatively funded project of the province, Nature Trust of B.C., The Nature Conservancy of Canada and certain American entities. The Centre keeps a computerized data bank on habitats, plants and animals, rare or at risk. Three rare plants under observation include Lyle's mariposa lily, Tweed's rock rose and Raup's willow. Contact the Conservation Data Centre, Wildlife Branch, Ministry of Water, Land and Air Protection, 780 Blanshard St., Victoria, V8V 1X5, (250) 356-0928, or (604) 299-9000 ext. 3825.

The Steelhead Society of British Columbia battles to save steelhead, a type of salmon-trout. Dismal steelhead returns seem to mark the demise of this species as massive U.S. and Canadian fleets of commercial netters, targeting enhanced runs of pink and sockeye salmon, accidentally kill 15,000 to 30,000 returning Skeena steelhead. In 1991, several Nass and Skeena river guides could not find a single fish, and sent visiting clients home in record numbers.

Steelhead are the tip of the iceberg as Canadian and American fishers share bleak tales of once-plentiful wild salmon stocks. *The Economist* magazine noted an event unchanged in 100 years. On the eve of the year 1900, British Columbia and Washington/Alaska were arguing over counting and preserving fish stocks. The quest for a workable international treaty remains an ongoing problem.

Another complicated issue is that of logging. This not only disturbs forests, but streams and the salmon that depend on them. Clearcutting accelerates erosion and turns streambeds muddy; logs yarded across streams disturb fine gravel harboring spawning eggs and fry; logging debris clogs channels, preventing adult fish from migrating upstream. The Sierra Legal Defense Fund has launched a Salmon Habitat Protection Project to help a concerned public protect salmon streams. Sloppy practices are under intense scrutiny and through increased enforcement, they are now reduced.

The Government of British Columbia faces a difficult task. While it must be committed to protecting and restoring the quality and integrity of the environment, reality dictates that its regulations and laws limit a prosperous economy for present and future generations. The concerns of individuals and communities must be respected even as environmental and economic needs are balanced.

The abundant natural resources of BC's forests make social, economic and environmental issues of vital importance to each one of us who uses and enjoys the great outdoors. Humans remain the only species capable of ignoring what is easy and exercising difficult options. Only humans can protect and preserve the environment.

Features & Attractions

Dr. Sun Yat-Sen Classical Chinese Garden

Vancouver offers an exciting and diverse range of attractions. Whether you're interested in the arts scene, public parks and gardens, marine life or things to do with kids, your visit to this dynamic city will be a memorable one. The following are some of the best-loved features.

Vancouver Sightseeing

Downtown and West End Highlights

Bloedel Floral Conservatory is an exotic enclosed dome, a world of jungle plants and desert vegetation with free-flying tropical birds located in Queen Elizabeth Park near Quarry Gardens. Admission. Phone (604) 257-8570 or (604) 299-9000, extension 5055.

Canada Place and CN IMAX combine outstanding views of Vancouver with a theatre featuring a giant screen that is five stories high, and wraparound IMAX digital sound. Both regular IMAX and IMAX 3-D films seem to pull you into the picture. IMAX is a Canadian technology now earning worldwide acclaim; #201, 999 Canada Place, north end, (604) 682-2384 or (604) 299-9000, extension 3213. Admission.

Dr. Sun Yat-Sen Classical Chinese Garden is a Ming dynasty scholar's garden, one acre in size, and one of the only authentic Chinese gardens outside of Asia. Guided tours and special events are common; 578 Carrall St., (604) 662-3207. Admission.

Granville Island offers arty shopping in addition to a huge fresh food market. Among its treasures are bakeries, shops, BC crafts, art galleries, artisans, theatres, fishing charters, kayak rentals and a children's water park. Street entertainment and seasonal festivals complement busy city views; 1667 Duranleau St. (604) 299-9000. Admission is free; parking is difficult.

H.R. Macmillan Planetarium and the Pacific Space Centre present journeys through space and time from the comfort of an armchair. Several daily star showings are pro-

jected onto a 20 m (66 foot) dome. Also featured are evening laser light shows with rock music; 1100 Chestnut St., (604) 738-7827, 738-STAR, or (604) 299-9000, extension 3214. Admission.

Harbour Cruises presents daily Port of Vancouver tours, sunset dinner cruises, boat-train day trips, or daily paddle-wheeler tours; #1 north foot of Denman St., (604) 688-7246 or 1-800-663-1500. Further information at 299-9000 ext.3214. Cost varies with services chosen.

Vancouver Champagne Cruises,(604) 688-6625, has a two-hour sunset Dinner Cruise around English Bay on a yacht, #100-1676 Duranleau St. Fyrther info at (604) 299-9000 ext. 2628.

Vancouver Harbour Tours, 1-800-667-0882, has a 75 min. tour of Burrard Inlet past Stanley Park, Lions Gate Bridge, the busy cruise ship terminals, the spectacular city skyline and the breathtaking North ShoreMountains aboard the M.P.V. Constitution Paddlewheeler.

Paddlewheeler River Adventures offers scenic Vancouver cruises and charters on the Fraser River and surrounding west coast waters. Moored in New Westminster Quay Public Market and one block from the New Westminster Skytrain Station, (604) 525-4465 or 1-877-825-1302. Further info at (604) 299-9000 ext. 4465.

Lookout! Viewing Deck at Harbour Centre offers a picture perfect 360-degree view from the top of a tower plus a video theatre, cappuccino service and friendly guides . Stop in at the Skylift at 555 West Hastings St., (604) 689-0421 or (604) 299-9000, ext. 2626. Admission.

Nitobe Japanese Garden is an authentic Japanese stroll and tea garden about 2.5 acres in size; near 6393 NW Marine Drive, (604) 822-6038 or (604) 299-9000 ext. 9666. Admission.

Science World & Alcan OMNIMAX is a place where innovative displays allow visitors to walk on sound, blow square

Quirky Facts

In the year 1900, British author Rudyard Kipling arrived for an extended visit in fledgling Victoria and Vancouver. He was completely enamoured. He felt British Columbia would be the most wonderful place to live … in about 50 years.

British architect Sir Francis Mawson Rattenbury, whose buildings are considered sensible with romantic overtones, designed Victoria's Parliament Buildings and the Empress Hotel, as well as Vancouver's courthouse, which now serves as the Vancouver Art Gallery. However, he is most famous in the UK for his news-making demise. In 1920, he was murdered at the hands of his young wife (suspiciously found innocent), ably assisted by the chauffeur (found guilty). His wife subsequently committed suicide.

Albert Cadman, the Marine Building's superintendent during the 1950s, once fell down the elevator shaft. The man who was sent to revive him with a glass of brandy took one look at the battered body, drank the brandy himself and fainted. Cadman recovered completely.

Vancouver is the only major city in Canada that was not established as a Hudson's Bay Co. fur trading post. The first significant non-native settlement occurred during the 1854-65 rush for gold—the Fraser River Stampede, followed by the 1863 Cariboo Gold Rush. It boomed in 1859 with the discovery of coal near today's Stanley Park, and again after 1889, when Vancouver became the terminus of the Canadian Pacific Railway.

When 20-year-old Gastown was first surveyed in 1870, it was a collection of unfinished wagon trails, squalid tar shacks, three saloons, two stores, one hotel and crude log wharves. Among its residents were squalling children, half-mad dogs and many Hawaiians, known locally as Kanakas. Captain Stamp, the resident magistrate, declared upon seeing his new charge, "What is the meaning of this aggregation of filth?"

Today, more than 2,800 ships flying the flags of more than 60 nations slip under the Lion's Gate Bridge each year to dock in Port of Vancouver, one of the busiest ports on the Pacific coast of the Americas.

The air-supported double-membrane Teflon roof over BC Place Stadium was first inflated in 1982. The patented technique has been compared to a tennis racket in the way it distributes stress. There is enough concrete in the stadium to build a sidewalk from Vancouver to Tacoma, Washington.

left: Stanley Park overview

Horseshoe Bay

bubbles or see optical illusions. Besides galleries full of experimental fun, regular showings of a spectacular IMAX film are projected onto one of the world's largest theatre dome screens; 1455 Quebec St. and Terminal Avenue, (604) 268-6363 or (604) 299-9000, extension 3211. Admission. Parking fees are in effect. Allow three hours.

Stanley Park Horse-drawn Tours are approximately 50 minutes in length with tours departing from the information booth at the lower "zoo" parking lot approximately every half-hour from May 1 to October 15. Vehicles seat up to 20 passengers. No reservations are required. Admission, (604) 681-5115.

U.B.C. Botanical Garden is set in a 70-acre coastal forest and features exotic plants from around the world. Most notable are its alpine garden, rhododendron gardens, physick garden and Asian gar-

dens; 6804 SW Marine Drive, (604) 822-4186 or (604) 299-9000, extension 9666. Admission is about $4.50.

U.B.C. Museum of Anthropology features award-winning displays of totem poles and West Coast Native arts and artifacts as well as Pacific Rim countries; 6393 NW Marine Drive, U.B.C. Campus (604) 822-5087 or (604) 299-9000, extension 3825. Admission.

Vancouver Aquarium Marine Science Centre in Stanley Park features more than 8,000 animals and fishes from around the world in Canada's largest aquarium. This facility is open 365 days a year, and is located inside the park entrance, (604) 659-3474, 604 268-9900, or (604) 299-9000, extension 3210. Admission. There is a fee for parking. Allow two to three hours.

Vancouver Art Gallery offers changing exhibits of historical and contemporary arts;

750 Hornby St. (604) 662-4709. The permanent collection features the work of Emily Carr. Admission; Thursday evenings, visitors pay by donation from 5 p.m. to 9 p.m.

Vancouver Maritime Museum is a showcase for regional and world ship history and features an outdoor antique boat display on the dock. Also included are guided tours of the first boat to navigate the famed Northwest Passage, the *St. Roch*; 1905 Ogden, (604) 257-8300 or (604) 299-9000, extension 2212. Admission.

Vancouver Museum showcases permanent and revolving exhibits with an emphasis on regional history; Vanier Park, 1100 Chestnut St. Admission. Phone (604) 737-2621 or (604) 299-9000, extension 4431. Closed Mondays.

VanDusen Botanical Garden is a 55-acre display of spectacular blooms and flowering trees. The sprawling grounds include dramatic rock landscaping, tranquil lakes, panoramic views and a maze garden. This is Vancouver's finest show garden; parking is free; 5251 Oak St. at 37th, (604) 878-9274. Admission.

Yacht charters are available from a number of companies including **Westin Bayshore Yacht Charters**, 1601 West Georgia St., (604) 691-6936. Contact the Vancouver tourist information centre, (604) 683-2000 for a complete list.

North Shore Sightseeing Highlights

A 61-acre waterfront area with beaches, fishing, sports facilities and pitch-and-putt golfing, **Ambleside Beach**'s highlight is a picturesque two-mile-long Seawall.

British Properties Drive About, starting on the north end of Taylor Way, winds its way through a parcel of land originally purchased for $30,000 by the (Irish) Guinness brewing family. They also built the Lions Gate Bridge in a grateful but Depression-weary city. Since the late 1930s, British Properties has been Vancouver's most prestigious neighbourhood. The community's solidly upper-income, overtaxed inhabitants enjoy spectacular city views, proximity to downtown Vancouver, golf and country clubs, while remaining comfortably ensconced. Homes in Lower British Properties average $550,000 to $800,000 and in Upper British Properties, $1 million to over $1.5 million.

A pleasant, secluded seaside community located at the gateway to Howe Sound, the quaint centre of **Horseshoe Bay** is complemented by a marina, a major BC Ferries terminal, a pretty park and views of the surrounding islands.

Capilano Salmon Hatchery, located in the Capilano River Regional Park, is an architecturally designed enhancement facility deep in a cedar forest. It illustrates the life cycle of the salmon, and is open to the public. It is located at 4500 Capilano Park Road, North Vancouver; please follow the signs; (604) 666-1790. Admission is free.

Capilano Suspension Bridge and Park offers a thrilling adventure 70 m (230 feet) above the Capilano River. Cross the swinging footbridge, then meander along short trails through the West Coast rainforest. Watch native totem pole carvers at work and visit the Canadiana gift shop. Parking is free, 20 minutes from downtown Vancouver; 3735 Capilano Road, North Vancouver, (604) 985-7474, or (604) 299-9000, extension 7000. Admission.

Grouse Mountain—The Peak of Vancouver is 15 minutes from downtown Vancouver and offers a mountaintop playground with panoramic vistas of Vancouver all the way to Vancouver Island. Enjoy casual or fine dining, an exciting sports movie, Logger Sport Shows, the Peak Chairlift or a Children's Adventure playground. The mountaintop Hiwus Feast House provides an authentic First Nations Dining experience. Phone (604) 984-0661 or (604) 299-9000, exten-

North Shore

In 1863, Mr. Sewell Moody, a Maine-born lumberman, bought a sawmill on Vancouver's North Shore. With the mill thriving, the settlement around the mill came to be called "Moodyville." Sewell and his family then purchased a beachfront home in elegant Victoria on Vancouver Island. On November 4, 1875, Moody boarded a steamer bound for San Francisco. Off Cape Flattery, the SS *Pacific* sank. For weeks, drowned bodies washed ashore; Moody was not one of the two survivors. Many months later, a spooky piece of wooden debris from the ship washed up within a stone's throw of his family home. In his distinctive handwriting the plank read, "S.P. Moody. All Lost."

North Vancouver's main street, Lonsdale Avenue, was named after an early bank

financier. It was once used to skid logs felled along the mountainsides down to the water and then onto the sawmills. Since there was work available near such places, tents and temporary dwellings sprang up alongside this "corduroy road." In time, it was called "Skid Road."

During the 1860s the only medical help was a "nurse" who refused to live in rowdy saloon-infested Gastown. When her help was needed, someone would hoist a signal-flag and she would row from her North Shore home, across the inlet to Gastown.

During the 1970s West Vancouver used to boast the highest per capita income in Canada. However, in recent years at $49,223 per person, it has fallen to 6th place—well behind several Ontario municipalities.

sion 6611. Admission.

A magnificent waterfront park with gigantic Sitka spruce trees, **Lighthouse Park** features an active lighthouse and kilometres of splendid hiking trails.

Lynn Canyon Ecology Centre and Suspension Bridge, 3663 Park Road off Peters Road, North Vancouver, (604)981-3103, is a free suspension bridge.

Maplewood Farm is a 2 ha (5 acre) park that the little ones love. It is home to ducks, lambs, chickens, billy goats and all the fluffy rabbits you can imagine. Take the Deep Cove exit to 405 Seymour River Place, North Vancouver, (604) 929-5610. Admission.

Park and Tilford Gardens features 2.5 acres groomed into a series of theme garden "rooms" including Asian, herb, colonnade, rose garden, native and white gardens; #440, 333 Brooksbank Avenue, North Vancouver, (604) 984-8200. Admission is free.

Fireworks illuminate Vancouver's skyline

Symphony of Fire

During late July and early August, three nations noted for their fireworks companies are invited to Vancouver to compete from a long sand-covered barge moored in English Bay. First, each nation has a night to itself. Radio stations play choreographed music and each fireworks company mounts its best performance. On the fourth night, the finale, all three competitors display in succession. International judges choose a winner.

Crowds estimated at over 350,000 watch from every possible vantage point along the shoreline. Charter boats also view the show from the water. Displays begin about 10:15 p.m., last about 30 minutes and those attending are urged to use public transit. Extra SkyTrain runs are planned and buses operate on five-minute schedules.

Past competitors in the Symphony of Fire have included France, the United States, the United Kingdom, Spain and China. There are about 100 top fireworks manufacturers in the world.

Each competitor carefully prepares a characteristic show complete with matching music. Spain, for example, is noted for its showy cascading bursts of glittering gold dust. The Chinese team, chosen from several fireworks companies in their home country, called their last presentation Fant'Asia. Meant to represent various countries, it began with silver fireworks for Japan, then gold for Mongolia, and finally, the warm colours of Tibet. In 1997, the winning Chinese team competed in five international festivals; four of them were in Canada.

Vancouver's Favourite Festivals by Date

Open to the public. Phone for details, (604) 299-9000, extension 3232.

Name	Events	Where	When
Polar Bear Swim	Plunge into ocean and get a commemorative button	English Bay	New Year's Day, 2:30 p.m.
Chinese New Year Celebrations, (604) 682-2222	Fireworks, calligraphy displays, dragon dances, parade, costumes	Various venues, West Pender St.	late January for one or two days
Vancouver Playhouse International Wine Festival, (604) 872-6622	Gala dinner and auction, public wine tastings, industry competitions	Vancouver Trade & Convention Centre, various venues	March or April for five days
Dancing on the Edge Festival, (604) 689-0926	Dance performances, workshops, some free performances	Firehall Arts Centre and various venues	late April for two days
Hyack Festival, (604) 522-6894	Family entertainment, exploding anvil salute, sporting activities, old cars	New Westminster, various venues	mid-May for nine days
World Championship Cup Dragon Boat Festival, (604) 669-1888	International and local team competitions, performing and visual arts, food festival	Concorde Pacific Place, False Creek, Plaza of Nations	mid-June for nine days
duMaurier International Jazz Festival, (604) 872-5200	More than 240 international & local jazz groups, individual performers, improvisations, free & ticket performances	Various venues	mid- to late June for 10 days
Bard on the Beach (604) 737-0625	Professional summer Shakespeare Festival	Tents in Vanier Park on English Bay	June until September
Canada Day Celebrations, (604) 666-7200	Fireworks, official citizenships, various activities	Canada Place	July 1st
Dancing on the Edge Festival (604)280-3311	Dance performances, workshops, some free performances	Firehall Arts Centre and various venues	2 weekends in early July
Vancouver Folk Music Festival, (604) 602-9798	Theme concerts, groups and individual performances, workshops	Jericho Beach Park and Granville Island	mid-July for three days
Vancouver International Comedy Festival,(604) 683-0883	National and international comedy performers of all types	Granville Island, various venues	late July for 11 days
Early Music Festival (604)732-1610	Music from the Middle Ages through the late Romantic era	UBC Recital Hall	Late July to mid August
Symphony of Fire, Vancouver Fireworks Society, (604) 738-4304	International teams of fireworks manufacturers compete for top honours	English Bay	late July, start of four staggered performances
Caribbean Day Festival, (604) 275-0233	Caribbean music, food, dancing, steel drums	Waterfront Park, Lonsdale Quay	late July for one day
Vancouver Chamber Music Festival, (604) 602-0363	Prelude concerts, picnics, classical events	Crofton House School, Vanier Park	late July for 12 days
Powell Street (Japanese) Festival, (604) 739-9388	Japanese-Canadian festival, origami, food, martial arts, dancing, kids' events	Oppenheimer Park, 400 block Powell St.	early August for two days
Fringe Festival, (604) 257-0350	500 theatre and performing artists, outdoor street performers, food	Commercial Drive, various venues	early September for 11 days
Vancouver International Film Festival, (604) 685-0260	300 feature films and shorts from 45 countries, guest stars, trade forum	Various theatres	early October for up to 17 days
Vancouver International Writers Festival, (604) 681-6330	Readings, international and Canadian authors, discussions	Granville Island	late October for five days
Christmas at Hycroft, University Women's Club of Vancouver, (604) 731-4661	Heritage house decorated for Christmas, craft fair, music performances	McRae Mansion, 1489 McRae Ave.	early to mid-November for three days

Vancouver's Biggest Consumer Trade Shows by Date

All listed shows are open to the public. Phone for details. Many (but not all) trade shows are held in facilities run by the BC Pavilion Corp. For up-to the-minute information, call the recording at the Event Line, (604) 661-7373.

Name/Contact	Exhibits	Where	Month
Vancouver Fishing & Outdoor Show, (604) 683-4766	Fishing, tackle, hunting, boats, camping, lodges and resorts	PNE Food Forum Buildings	January
Pacific International Auto Show, (604) 214-9964	New models of cars, light trucks, sport utility vehicles, and after-market accessories and services	BC Place Stadium, (604) 669-2300	January
Vancouver International Motorcycle Show, (905) 470-6123	New, vintage, custom motorcycles, lifestyle, after-market accessories & services	PNE Food Forum Buildings, (604) 253-2311	January
BC Home & Garden Show, (604) 433-5121	Home improvement, renovations, gardening, landscaping	BC Place Stadium	February
Vancouver International Boat Show, (604) 294-1313	Consumer boat show, models, services, products	BC Place Stadium	February
Vancouver International RV Show & Sales, (604) 533-4200	Recreational vehicle models; after-market accessories and services, lifestyles, travel	BC Place Stadium	February
Fraser Valley Boat and Sportsmen's Show, (604) 683-4766	Fishing, hunting, camping & outdoor recreational gear, lodges and resorts	Tradex-Fraser Valley Trade & Exhibition Centre	March
The Wellness Show, (604) 520-7168	Health, nutrition, physical activity, recreation, leisure	Vancouver Trade & Convention Centre	February
VanDusen Garden Show, (604) 257-8671	Outdoor show, sample gardens, nursery landscaping, services, accessories	VanDusen Botanical Garden	June
Aerospace North America, (604) 852-4600	Biannual aviation and aerospace trade show	Tradex-Fraser Valley Trade & Exhibition Centre	August every second year:2003, 2005 etc.
Vancouver Coal Harbour Floating Boat Show (604) 683-2628	Boats	Coal Harbour	September
BC Home Show, (604) 412-2288	Home improvements, renovations	BC Place Stadium	October
Vancouver Ski Snow Show, (604) 878-0754	Skiing, snowboarding, clothing & equipment, resorts, winter vehicles	BC Place Stadium	October
Lower Mainland Dog Fanciers Show, (604) 599-6992	Breed championships, dog show & obedience trials	Tradex-Fraser Valley Trade & Exhibition Centre	October
Circle Craft Christmas Market, (604) 801-5220	Hand-crafted articles by the artisans, homemade preserves and candies	Vancouver Trade and Convention Centre	November

Lighthouse Park

Special Interest Sightseeing

Architectural Tours of Vancouver are scheduled in the summer; check for current departures and starting points (usually in Gastown). The tour guides are architecture students; admission is free, #100, 440 Cambie St., Vancouver, (604) 683-8588.

The Canadian Craft Museum has revolving displays dedicated to excellence in crafts and design. Located a block from the Vancouver Art Gallery, the gift shop here is a real find; Cathedral Place Courtyard, 639 Hornby St., Vancouver, (604) 687-8266. Admission.

Forest Alliance of BC has displays dedicated to explaining BC's forests and sustainable development. It is open to the public, and there are free posters, brochures on forestry, walking tours and mill tours as well as tree seedling kits. Plaza Level, 1200 1130 W. Pender St., Vancouver, (604) 685-7507 or 299-900, extension 7507. Admission is free.

Kitsilano Showboat is a fascinating Vancouver tradition. Tap dancing and ballet school graduates as well as energetic amateurs with all manner of silly theatricals strut their best dancing and singing performances on an outdoor stage by the water; outdoor amphitheatre at 2300 Cornwall, Vancouver. Check for the latest program; (604) 734-7332. Admission is minimal.

Museum of the Exotic World features displays from large insects to stuffed crocodiles; 3271 Main St., Vancouver; (604) 876-8713. Open Saturday and Sunday only; admission is free.

Roedde House Museum is one of the grand old mansions from Vancouver's early days; Sunday tea and tours, concerts; 1415 Barclay St., Vancouver, (604) 684-7040. Admission.

TRIUMF Tour is all about sub-atomic particles including muons, pions and other minuscule bits of atoms generated for experimental purposes in a world-class physics facility; call ahead for guided tour times. It is located at the south end of Westbrook Mall on U.B.C. campus, Vancouver (604) 222-1047. Note: This tour involves climbing many flights of stairs. Admission is free.

Vancouver Police Centennial Museum, the best police museum in Canada, it has some bizarre and unusual displays on the hilarious history of crime in rip roarin' Vancouver. Features include a peek at a morgue; 240 E. Cordova, Vancouver, (604) 665-3346. Admission.

Vancouver Public Library is an architectural masterpiece built roughly in the shape of the Roman Coliseum spiraling open like a giant snail shell. Now a wonder in itself, visitors come to marvel at its form. Periodic guided tours are offered; 635 Georgia St., Vancouver, (604) 331-3600.

Canadian Venture Exchange Visitors & Investors Centre offers a self-guided tour, information on the history of the exchange, and a computerized hookup to the trading floor. Special tour presentations are available; 609 Granville St., Vancouver (604) 643-6590. Admission is free.

The Abbotsford International Airshow (604) 852-8511, Abbotsford International Airport, is a 3-day event in August set in the Fraser Valley with Mt. Baker as a backdrop. It is attended by over 200,000 people and host representatives from approximately 25 countries including Ambassadors, Consuls General, and Military Attaches. Most major airshow performers and military demonstration teams have performed here, including the CAF Snowbirds, USAF Thunderbirds, USN Blue Angels, Patrouille de France, Frecci Tricilori (Italy) Chile and the Russian Knights.

Vancouver With Kids

Stanley Park With Kids
Bayshore Bicycles and Rollerblade Rentals, near Stanley Park, Westin Bayshore Hotel or 745 Denman St., (604) 688-2453, has all sizes of wheels: Cost is about $ 5.50 per hour for either bikes or blades; an all-day rate is available.

Second Beach or Third Beach in Stanley Park, Park

Third Beach

Drive near 2099 Beach Ave., (604) 257-8400 or (604) 299-9000 ext. 4100, includes a salt water pool, playground and spray water park. Parking and lockers cost a small fee.

Stanley Park boat rentals, 1525 Coal Harbour Quay, (604) 682-6257, rents 15, 16 or 17 foot motorized boats complete with safety equipment.

Stanley Park horse-drawn tours, (604) 681-5115, are approximately 50 minutes in length. Tours depart from the information booth at the lower "zoo" parking lot approximately every half hour from March 15 to October 31. Vehicles seat up to 20 passengers. No reservations are required.

Stanley Park Petting Zoo (604) 257-8531, Farmyard, Water Park and Miniature Train are popular attractions. Please

note: if you have a car, it is not necessary to walk among all these facilities. There are pay parking lots near each location.

Stanley Park Pitch & Putt, 2099 Beach Ave, Stanley Park, (604) 681-8847, is a par three course in a beautiful setting.

Vancouver Aquarium Marine Science Centre, Stanley Park, (604) 659-3508, features more than 8,000 animals and fish in Canada's largest aquarium. Its stars are the ever-popular beluga and killer whales. This facility is located just inside the park entrance. Admission. There is a fee for parking.

Rainy Days With Kids
Aquadventures Swim Centre, 1630 West 5th Ave. near Fir, (604) 736-SWIM, is a special pool with warm water and wide, gradual steps for young-

sters. Also suitable for persons with disabilities. Phone for public swim times.

Canada Place and CN IMAX, 999 Canada Place, (604)682-2384, combine outstanding exterior views of Vancouver with a theatre featuring a giant screen that is five stories high and wraparound IMAX digital sound. Both regular IMAX and IMAX 3-D films put you in the picture. IMAX is a Canadian technology now earning worldwide acclaim. Admission.

H.R. Macmillan Planetarium, 1100 Chestnut St., (604) 738-7827 or (604) 299-9000 ext. 3214, features journeys through space and time from the comfort of an armchair. There are several star showings daily and evening laser light shows with rock music. Admission is about $4, less for children.

Kids Only World at Granville Island is a favourite stop.

Lonsdale Quay Ball Room, 123 Carrie Cates Court, at the foot of Lonsdale Avenue, North Vancouver, is for little ones under eight years of age. It is a room filled with coloured ping pong balls. Adjacent are several kids' stores. It can be accessed easily via the exciting public transit Sea Bus. Call for information on the transit Sea Bus, (604) 985-6261.

McDonald's restaurants have brightly coloured playgrounds associated with many of their fast food restaurants. If you wish to know about where the biggest and best indoor playgrounds are located, contact Community Relations at (604) 294-2181.

Newton Wave Pool, 13730 72nd Ave., Surrey, (604) 501-5540 or (604) 299-9000, extension 5540, generates huge,

crashing indoor waves, has two water slides, a wading pool and lagoon, a toddler pool, a whirlpool and is considered the "Big Kahuna" for family fun. Admission.

Granville Island Model Ships, Model Trains & Sport Fishing Museums, 1502 Duranleau, Granville Island, (604) 683-1939. This is actually a collection of three museums. Most of their displays are down low so smaller kids will have no difficulty seeing what there is to see. The Model Ships Museum houses over 50 models of vessels. The Model Trains Museum has a large international collection of trains that weave around tracks, through tunnels, along cliffs and across trestles. The Sport Fishing Museum has an extensive collection including a simulator where you can try to wrestle a 35 pound Spring Salmon to the boat.

Children's Festivals

These festivals are little ones' favourites. Some are dedicated to children. Others have children's components. Phone for details or updated information at (604) 299-9000, extension 3232.

Name/Contact	Events	Where	When
La Fête Colombienne des Enfants, (604) 535-1311	Children's events in French	Coquitlam	Late April for 3 days
Hyack Festival, (604)522-6894	Family entertainment, exploding anvil salute, fun run, sporting activities, old cars	New Westminster, various venues	Mid-May for 9 days
Vancouver Int'l. Children's Festival, (604)708-5655	Famous performers, music, dance, art, storytelling for ages 4 to 16.	Vanier Park in big-top tents	Late May for 7 days
Canada Day Celebrations, (604) 666-7200	Fireworks, various activities	Canada Place	July first
Caribbean Day Festival, (604) 275-0233	Caribbean music, food, dancing, steel drums	Waterfront Park, Lonsdale Quay	Late July for 1 day
Powell Street Festival, (604) 739-9388	Japanese-Canadian festival, origami, food, martial arts, dancing, kid's events	Oppenheimer Park, 400 block Powell St.	Early August for 2 days
Fringe Festival, (604) 257-0350 Check suitability for age group.	500 theatre and performing artists, outdoor street performers, food	Commercial Drive, various venues	Early September for 11 days
Coquitlam Children's Festival,	Children's musical shows, activities, storytelling, clowning	Town Centre, Coquitlam	Second weekend in September

Rainforest Reptile Refuge Society, 1395-176 St. in Surrey, (604) 538-1711, is a permanent shelter for unwanted, abused and abandoned reptiles and amphibians. Admission.The Refuge is a non-profit organization that provides an appropriate habitat for a variety of exotic animals.

Science World, 455 Quebec St., (604) 268-6363 or 299-9000 ext. 3211, has hundreds of interactive displays for kids. Highlights include: shows exploring different scientific principles in creative and fun ways, interactive displays for kids of all ages, live habitats featuring the lives of bees, snakes, frogs, insects and geckos.

Gator Pit, Park Royal, West Vancouver (604) 608-6699, is a softplay parkwith nets, tunnels and ball pit.

Vancouver Aquarium Marine Science Centre in Stanley Park, (604) 659-3474 or (604) 299-9000, extension 3210, features over 8,000 animals and fish in Canada's largest aquarium. The stars are the ever-popular beluga whales, dolphins and seals. Also ask about times for special three-hour kids' programs. Admission. Parking requires a fee. Allow two to three hours.

Vancouver Art Gallery, 750 Hornby Street, (604) 299-9000, extension 5621, has a bonus on the third Sunday of every month when the Gallery is transformed into a fun-filled learning environment for families with school-aged children. Activities include hands-on art, drop-in studios, interpretive performances, guided tours and art demonstrations. A fee is charged; Thursday

Kitsilano Beach Park and pool

nights are the least expensive.

Vancouver Kidsbooks, 3040 Edgemont Blvd., North Vancouver (604) 986-6190, is a specialty store for kids, teachers, and parents and also has an excellent selection of videos, cassettes, cards and gift wrap.

Vancouver Maritime Museum, 1905 Ogden Ave., (604) 299-9000, extension 2212, or (604) 257-8300, has special programs for kids. Past programs have included "Shipwreck Disasters" or "Sail Away With Me." Best for ages 10 and up.

Waterfront Theatre, 1410 Cartwright St., (604) 685-6217, is home to the Carousel Theatre and offers outstanding children's theatre and other lighthearted productions. Phone for current presentations.

Sunny or Partly Cloudy Days With Kids

Airplanes whoosh by overhead, creating loud noises, searing turbulence and downdrafts. A special **airplane-viewing park**, with miniature replicas of historical airplanes,

picnic benches and a restroom, is located at the end of the runway at Airport Road and Russ Baker Way. Admission is free.

Family Fun on a boat is great way to spend an afternoon. Rent your own 14, 15, or 16 foot motorized fiberglass boat by the hour and explore nearby islands and coves; safety equipment is provided. Reserve ahead, (604) 921-3474, then drive to **Sewell's Landing**, 6695 Nelson Ave., Horseshoe Bay, West Vancouver for a great family adventure.

Festivals can include all sorts of free demonstration performances from sample bicycle races to fringe comedy routines and live jazz. Ask about the Harrison Festival, (604) 796-3664; July First fireworks at Canada Place, (604) 666-8477; or the July sandcastle competition at Spanish Banks, (604) 257-8140. Call (604) 299-9000, or Tourism Vancouver, (604) 683-2000. Alternatively, call the Granville Island Information Centre, (604) 666-5784.

Kids Market on Granville Island

Special Treat for Kids

Combine these adventures every which way.

• Royal Hudson Day Trip is a 90-minute, one-way trip through a spectacular mountain-ocean vista via a real old fashioned steam train. Runs from June to September. Check the total duration of return trip with a stopover. For reservations and departure times from North Vancouver, call BC Rail at (604) 984-5246.

• Train-Boat day trip is a combination of the Royal Hudson Steam Train, listed above, with a return journey via a 500-passenger ocean-going vessel MV *Britannia*. Make your day

adventure complete. Reservations are required. Contact Harbour Cruises, (604) 688-7246.

• Train & Boat & Whistler Resort! Combine ocean going boat, Royal Hudson Steam Train and motor-powered coach with an overnight excursion to Whistler, a really efficient way to see mountains, ocean and a world-famous ski and summer resort the kids love. In the summer, there are lots of young people skateboarding, bicycling and enjoying the outdoors. Contact Pacific Spirit Tours, (604) 683-0209 or 1-888-286-8722.

Granville Island offers an outdoor **Children's Water Park** and a **Kids Only Market**, 1667 Duranleau St., (604) 299-9000, as well as a huge fresh food market, bakeries, shops, street entertainment, seasonal festivals and city views. Admission is technically free. Parking is difficult.

Greater Vancouver Zoological Centre, 5048-264th Street, Aldergrove, (604) 856-6825 or 299-9000 ext. 6825, has over 840 animals including bears, rhinos, tigers and baby animals on 120 acres of farmland on the far outskirts of the city. Ride the Safari Express.

Jericho Beach Park, north foot of Discovery St., (604) 257-8400, has a large beach and park area encompassing 45 ha (111 acres) that is excellent at sunset; bring a picnic and blankets. Admission is free.

Kitsilano Beach Park and Pool, north foot of Arbutus St., Vancouver, (604) 257-8400, charges admission to the pool at about $1 to $3 for kids.

Kitsilano Showboat, 2300 Cornwall, (604) 733-7297 or (604)734-7332, is a fascinating summer evening tradition. Tap dancing and ballet school graduates as well as martial arts schools and police dogs strut their best performances on an outdoor stage by the water. Check out the latest programs at this outdoor amphitheatre. Admission varies.

Maplewood Farm, 405 Seymour River Place, North Vancouver, (604) 929-5610, is a place the little ones love with ducks, lambs, chickens, billy goats, and all the fluffy rabbits you can imagine. Bring a picnic. They also offer periodic pony rides;. small admission.

39

Splashdown Waterpark Inc. Highway 17 at 52nd St., Tsawwassen near the BC Ferry Terminal, (604) 943-2251, offers a labyrinth of outdoor water slides;. Admission.

Vancouver With Older Kids

Forgotten in the "culture scenes" of some cities, older kids will love Vancouver.

Bayshore Bicycles and Rollerblade Rentals near Stanley Park, Westin Bayshore Hotel or 745 Denman St., (604) 688-2453, rents wheels Daily rates are available.

The BC Sports Hall of Fame and Museum, BC Place Stadium, Gate H, 777 Pacific Blvd. South, (604)687-5520, covers BC sports past and present. Displays include tributes to BC's wheelchair athlete Rick Hansen and hero Terry Fox. For older kids there are exercise machines, rowing machines and a place to calculate the speed of your baseball throw. Admission.

Discount Cinema Showtime has up-to-the-minute information at (604) 299-9000, extension 3456. For Vancouver movie show times, extension 3106;for children's video reviews, ext. 4322, for top videos, ext. 3091.

Ecomarine Ocean Kayak Centre, Duranleau St. on Granville Island, (604) 689-7575, offers fine half-day activities in the calm but interesting waters around Granville Island; inquire about age restrictions.

Kid City is a "most excellent" place to go and is covered under "Rainy Days with Kids."

Lynn Canyon Park and Suspension Bridge, 3366 Park Road, North Vancouver, (604)

Science Centre

981-3103, is a friendly rainforest wilderness complete with a heart-thumping suspension bridge 50 m (150 ft.) above a raging river. Considered a highlight by many, the trails take second place to the exciting suspension bridge. Daring 13- and 14-year-olds can bring their bathing suits if cliff jumping is their thing. Also on site is a small Ecology House with displays. Admission to all is free.

H.R. Macmillan Planetarium has evening light rock shows; see "Rainy Days with Kids."

Museum of the Exotic World, 3271 Main St., (604) 876-8713, features displays ranging from large beetles and insects to stuffed crocodiles and cannibalistic societies. This museum is a hit with kids who like to "gross their parents out." Admission is free.

Paintball or laser tag games are located on the outskirts of town. Maple Ridge has the best adrenaline outdoor paintball war fields and Surrey has the most serious laser games. Check out the yellow pages under "Paintball" for Planet Lazer, Splatter

Zone, Panther Paintball, Darkzone Laser, North West Paintball, Out of this World Entertainment, Colourwars. Costs vary.

Queen Elizabeth Pitch & Putt, 33rd & Cambie St., (604) 874-8336, is a par three course to while away a few delightful hours. Club rentals available.

Science World and Alcan OMNIMAX, 1455 Quebec St. and Terminal Avenue, (604)268-6363 or (604) 299-9000 ext. 3211, is a place where kids can walk on sound, blow square bubbles, see optical illusions and climb inside a hollow tree. Besides galleries full of experimental fun, regular showings of a spectacular IMAX film are projected onto the world's largest theatre dome screen; admission. Parking fees are in effect. Allow three to five hours.

Vancouver Police Centennial Museum, 240 E. Cordova, (604) 665-3346, the #1 police museum in Canada, has some bizarre and unusual displays on the hilarious history of crime in rip roarin' Vancouver. Features include a peek at a morgue; admission.

Beluga Whales

One of the most popular attractions at the Vancouver Aquarium is the beluga whale show. Relatively small whales, they have thick gray-white skin and a very thick blubber layer. Their flukes are flattened pads of tough, fibrous connective tissue, completely without bone. Belugas' most distinctive features are a fatty, oil-filled bump on their heads called a melon, and their lack of a dorsal fin. A dorsal fin would impede their ability to swim under ice to locate a breathing hole. Next to the *Orcinus orca* or killer whale, the beluga has become the most popular whale in the world.

The name "beluga" is derived from the Russian word *belukha,* which means "white"— an apt moniker for the world's only white whale. The Russians harvest its eggs and sell them as beluga caviar; ounce for ounce, it's a very expensive food.

Beluga whales are entirely arctic and sub-arctic, swimming slowly among ice floes. They inhabit the Arctic Ocean and large rivers such as Russia's Amur or Canada's Yukon and St. Lawrence. Some populations make southern migrations, while others remain in the same area year-round.

Perhaps the most friendly cetacean (aquatic mammal) species in the world, belugas are sociable, curious and spend much time near the surface.

Beluga whale

Belugas can bend the vertebrae in their necks and form their lips into a "smile." Though they do not exhibit aerial behaviors (jumping, breaching), they often swim up to boats.

Belugas are very vocal and can produce at least 11 sounds including high-pitched, resonant whistles, squeals, mews, chirps, trills and bell-like sounds. When alarmed, they cluck. All this gives rise to their nickname, "sea canary." They do not possess vocal cords; sound comes from air forced through the blowhole.

Belugas produce trains of rapid clicks. These bounce off objects, echo back, then pass through the melon—an acoustic lens that focuses the sound.

Normally slow swimmers, they amble in pods of 10 to 25 cohesive social individuals. They chase each other and rub together often. Belugas can submerge for 15 minutes but normally do five shallow dives followed by a one-minute deep dive. Their diet consists of octopus, squid, crabs, shrimp, clams,

snails and fishes. Belugas squirt water jets through their mouths to dislodge prey; they swallow everything whole. In zoological habitats, they eat three per cent of their body weight per day, about 18 to 30 kg (40-70 lb.)

Calves are born dark to brownish gray and upon reaching maturity at 8 to 10 years, they turn creamy white. After losing a newborn, adult belugas will carry objects on their backs to replace their lost offspring. First-time mothers learn how to nurse from other females, and calves nurse for a year until their teeth emerge.

Killer whales and polar bears prey on belugas that become trapped in the ice. Indigenous peoples of Canada, Alaska and Russia have always hunted them for meat, blubber and skin. Tanned beluga skin is the only cetacean skin thick enough for leather. The annual harvest is about 200 to 550 in Alaska and about 1,000 in Canada. Recently, industrial runoff in the St. Lawrence River has resulted in concentrations of toxins, which have killed many St. Lawrence River belugas.

Today's world population of belugas is estimated to be 62,000 to 80,000, each living 25 to 30 years. The beluga is listed in the IUCN World Conservation Union's "insufficiently known" category and is not protected.

Shopping & Strolling

Queen Elizabeth Park

Vancouver's astonishing variety of international influences makes a tour of its downtown core a truly cultural experience. One is struck by the success with which settlers from the "old world" have established their societies here. This makes the shopping unique and truly irresistible.

Driving Tour 1: Vancouver Downtown

The Vancouver Explorer covers the basic sights in about three to four hours, depending on traffic, and allows two 30-minute stops at the totem poles and Queen Elizabeth Park. Additional stops require additional time. Traffic in the core of Vancouver is heavy. Relax and be prepared to move slowly. This tour follows in the general path of guided sightseeing tours offered by sightseeing tour bus companies.

Start: Fairmont Hotel Vancouver, 900 West Georgia, heading east.

Check out the gargoyles perched high up on the 1930s **Fairmont Hotel Vancouver,** (604) 684-3131). Pass the Greco-Roman columnar facade of the Vancouver Art Gallery and Centennial Fountain, turn right on Howe St. and right again on Robson Street. Enjoying the crowds and shopping ambiance, turn right onto Denman St. At Georgia St., make a left, pass Lost Lagoon Fountain and enter **Stanley Park.** Upon entering the park, turn right. Passing by the Royal Vancouver Yacht Club, The **Vancouver Aquarium** is home to a captive killer whale and is hidden in the trees to the left. Stop at the **totem poles,** pay the parking

fee and have a closer look. These are real totem poles, mostly Kwakiutl in origin. Continue around to Brockton Point Lighthouse and past Lumberman's Arch, the tree sculpture. Circle around the park and stop at the **Hollow Tree** for a quick photograph. Continue past Second Beach and staying right, emerge from the park on Beach Ave.

Pass the waterfront apartments and Sunset Beach Park along the waterfront and travel to the Burrard Bridge. Turn right, cross the bridge and note the Salish hat-shaped building in Vanier Park. This is your next destination. The **H.R. MacMillan Planetarium, the Vancouver Museum,** the

left: Seawall in Stanley Park

A misty Stanley Park

adjacent **Vancouver Maritime Museum** (1905 Ogden, (604) 257-8300) and the **historic boat dock** may entice you to stop for a quick visit. Foot passenger ferries glide back and forth to Granville Island.

Emerge from the museum complex onto Cornwall Street, which winds in a westward direction along the south side of English Bay, through the Kitsilano District to the University of British Columbia. Follow the Scenic Route signs. Rounding Point Gray as it passes Kitsilano, Jericho and Locarno beaches, the street's name changes to Marine Drive. Stop for a quick gander at the architecturally resplendent **Museum of Anthropology,** 6393 N.W. Marine Drive, (604) 822-3825, and its totem poles. You can walk the outside grounds all the way around the museum; the ocean views are panoramic. For aficionados, the authentic Japanese Nitobe Memorial Garden is nearby. Continue on Marine Drive past U.B.C. Botanical Gardens

all the way to Cambie St. Turn right and head north to 33rd Avenue.

Turn right into **Queen Elizabeth Park,** a 53 ha (130 acre) mountain park with an arboretum on the way to the summit. Little Mountain is actually made of volcanic rock that juts out through the mass of glacial clay, sand and rocks that make up the bulk of Vancouver's sub-surface. Pay the parking fee and have a peek at Vancouver's skyline and the North Shore from the viewpoint. Visit **Quarry Gardens,** and stop in at **The Bloedel Floral Conservatory,** (604) 257-

8584. Admission is about $3.50.

Emerge from Little Mountain on Midlothian Drive and make your way back to Cam-

Alternate Vancouver Route

After crossing Cambie Bridge, drive immediately to Canada Place, 999 Canada Place, and find a parkade. This is a good starting point for a downtown walking tour or a quick walk over to The Landing for a visit to Gastown and Chinatown. Both Gastown and Chinatown are most interesting on foot.

No Car?

Public Transit Customer Information provides personalized assistance with schedules and routes, (604) 521-0400; or (604) 299-9000, extension 2233.

BC Public Transit routes are mapped out in this book and described in the BC Yellow Pages.

A Public Transit booklet describing all transit routes is available free or for $1 at all travel information centres, public libraries, 7-11 convenience stores, and chambers of commerce.

For bicycle information the listings.

RCMP at Canada Place

bie Street, travelling north. Pass near the tall, 1930s-style Vancouver City Hall on your way to Cambie Bridge. Crossing it, note **Science World,** which resembles a silver-golf-ball, and **BC Place Stadium,** the inflated-roof sports sta-

dium. See the alternative route suggestion at the end of this tour. Turn right on Beatty Street, travelling near the stadium to Pender Street. Turn left (west) and enjoy crawling through the spirited crowds in red coloured **Chinatown.** The

most interesting blocks are where the low 100s blocks change from East Pender to West Pender. Nearby is **Dr. Sun Yat-Sen Classical Chinese Garden,** 578 Carrall Street, a must-see for Asian garden aficionados. As you travel through Chinatown, Gastown parallels Chinatown two blocks to your right (north). You might want to double back to take in Gastown from end to end.

Watching one-way streets, make your way from Pender St. over to Water Street, travelling through the venerable old Gastown district. Gassy Jack's statue is located at the merging of Water, Carroll, Powell and Alexander streets across from the triangular-shaped Hotel Europe. Continue west past Waterfront Station, Water and Cordova, once the imposing gateway to the Orient and a terminus for the famous trans-continental Canadian Pacific Railway. Pass the white-sailed **Canada Place,** 999 Canada Place, home of the IMAX Theatre, where cruise ships dock throughout the summer. This completes your driving tour.

Driving Tour 2: North Shore Vistas

North Shore Vistas takes in the basic sights in about 4 to 5 hours and allows for short stops at Stanley Park's totem poles, Horseshoe Bay, the Capilano Salmon Enhancement Facility and the Capilano Suspension Bridge. Additional stops require additional time. This tour follows in the general path of guided sightseeing tours offered by tour bus companies. This tour is somewhat

Top Ten Vancouver Attractions

Vancouver Aquarium
in Stanley Park,: sightseeing
Granville Island Market,:
walking, shopping and eating
Gastown and Chinatown,:
walking and shopping
Queen Elizabeth Park and
Quarry Gardens,:
walking
Capilano Suspension Bridge &
Park in North Vancouver,:
walking

Lonsdale Quay Market,
North Vancouver,: shopping
and eating
Grouse Mountain—The Peak of
Vancouver,:
riding and walking
Lookout! at Harbour Centre,:
riding and sightseeing
CN IMAX Theatre,:
sightseeing and listening
Royal Hudson Steamtrain
Excursion,:
riding

less demanding on the driver than the Vancouver Driving Tour, though the distances are longer, in the neighbourhood of 60 km (40 miles) in total. Crossing the Lion's Gate bridge requires patience.

From downtown Georgia St., bear right into the 400 ha (1,000 acre) **Stanley Park.** Stop at the totem poles and take in the sails of Canada Place, and on the other side, the North Shore and its yellow sulphur exports. Continuing along the one-way Park Drive, take the Lions Gate Bridge exit (closed weekdays from 3:30 to 5:30 p.m.).

Cross the famous suspension bridge, an icon of Vancouver, and follow the signs to Highway 1. Continue about 15 km (10 miles) to the exit that leads to the picturesque village of **Horseshoe Bay** (HB) in West Vancouver. Stop and stroll HB's tiny downtown area along Waterfront Park as the ferries depart for Vancouver Island. Hungry? Try fish and chips from one of the waterfront restaurants or vendors.

Return along scenic Marine Drive, which winds its way past the Park Royal Shopping Centre to Capilano Road. Head left (north) toward the mountains, and at the 4500 block, make a left turn to **Capilano River Regional Park.** Here, deep in the fragrant cedar forest, are a salmon enhancement facility and a fish ladder. Visit the **Capilano Salmon Enhancement Facility.** Admission is free; parking requires a fee.

Continue up Capilano Road to the **Capilano Suspension Bridge,** 3735

Capilano Suspension Bridge

Capilano Road, (604) 985-7474, home to the world's highest suspension bridge. Stop to watch totem carvers at work, and discover the Canadiana gift shop. Walk awhile in the West Coast rainforest or take in a delicious salmon barbecue.

Continue up Capilano Road. Dam aficionados will want to park at **Cleveland Dam,** the structure regulating Vancouver's main water supply. A stroll across the top of the dam and a look down the

Royal Hudson Steam Train Excursions

Reservations are required for this popular way to view the spectacular ocean, mountain and forest vistas of coastal BC on fast-pace day excursions. Choose from 1) rail round trip, 2) rail and ocean, or 3) rail, ocean and Whistler Resort overnight… and back again!

The Royal Hudson Day Trip chugs through a spectacular mountain/ocean vista via an old fashioned, well-lubricated steam train. Runs from June through September. For reservations and departure times from North Vancouver, call BC Rail at (604) 984-5246.

Train-Boat day trip is a combination of the Royal Hudson Steam Train listed above with one way of the journey via a 500-passenger ocean-going vessel, MV *Britannia.* Make your round-trip adventure complete. It runs from June through September; reservations are required. Contact Harbour Cruises, (604) 688-7246 or (604) 299-9000, extension 9558.

Train & Boat & Whistler! Combine ocean-going MV *Britannia,* Royal Hudson Steam Train, and motorcoach with an overnight excursion to Whistler. This is a really efficient way to see the mountains, ocean and the world-famous alpine resort; Pacific Spirit Tours, (604) 683-0209 or 1-888-286-8722.

Grouse Mountain Skyride

spillway is a heart-thumping experience.

Continue up Capilano Road to its terminus at **Grouse**

Mountain—The Peak of Vancouver, 6400 Nancy Greene Way, (604) 980-9311 or 299-9000 ext. 6644. A scenic

ride in the **Skyride,** an aerial tram, takes visitors to an exciting mountaintop world including a brand new all-Native

Sightseeing Excursion Companies

Check out the various modes and pick one that suits you best. In addition to daily half- or full-day guided tours of Vancouver city highlights, many of these companies offer additional tours to 1) North Shore, Grouse Mountain and Capilano Suspension Bridge; 2) Victoria and The Butchart Gardens; or 3) Whistler and/or the Royal Hudson Steam Train.

Classic Limousine offers customized guided tours of Vancouver and the environs with small buses or limousines, (604) 267-1441.

Early Motion Tours Ltd. is a fun way to see Vancouver with a personal tour guide "in style" in a fine old, shiny Ford Model A

touring car; (604) 687-5088.

Gray Line of Vancouver offers frequent guided half- and full-day tours including Vancouver and mountain tours, Whistler day trips, or Victoria day excursions, (800) 667-0882, (604) 879-3363.

Landsea Tours runs daily guided sightseeing half- and full-day tours including Vancouver highlights, North Shore Mountains, Victoria and The Butchart Gardens, or Whistler. Big windows and clean white minicoaches with friendly service are a treat; (604) 255-7272.

Pacific Coach Lines offers frequent day trips to Victoria via large air-conditioned coaches; (800) 661-1725, or (604) 662-7575.

The Vancouver Trolley Company Ltd. offers a unique climb on, climb off day pass as their bright red trolleys crawl through the city, stopping at tourist highlights. A do-it-yourself tour, this takes more energy than a guided tour; phone for the nearest pick-up point; (604) 451-5581.

VIP Tourguide Services offers multilingual step-on services for local city tours, the Rockies, Alaska, Yellowstone and eastern Canada; (604) 214-4677.

West Coast City and Nature Sightseeing offers daily guided half- or full day-tours in English or German via 20- to 27-passenger mini-coaches; tours in French are offered by charter.

cuisine longhouse, Híwus, with traditional dancers; periodic Loggers' Sports Days; additional restaurants and cafés; paved mountain walking trails; chainsaw sculptures; helicopter sightseeing; hang gliding championships and recreational parasailing; and periodic movie or photographic presentations.

If you are not ascending Grouse Mountain the following is an alternative North Shore suggestion: From Grouse Mountain and Capilano Road, return to Highway 1, turn east and take the Lonsdale Ave. exit south to the waterfront. Enjoy a stop at **Lonsdale Quay Market,** 123 Carrie Cates Court at the foot of Lonsdale, North Vancouver, (604) 985-6261 or 299-9000 ext. 6261. This is a fresh food market with restaurants, gifts, roving entertainers, and views of downtown Vancouver. Some visitors like to let their families or companions cross back to the downtown via the public transport Sea Bus, (604) 521-0400. Its loading station adjoins the market. The driver can recover Sea Bus passengers in front of Waterfront Station, at the foot of Cordova and Water Street in Gastown. A Sea Bus ticket is low cost.

Make your way back across the Lion's Gate Bridge to downtown Vancouver.

Driving Tour 3: Raintree Garden Tour

The Raintree Garden Tour covers Vancouver's basic garden sights in about 4 to 6 hours and allows for short stops at Spanish Banks, the Museum of Anthropology Na-

Gardens of Stanley Park

tive Plant Garden, Nitobe Memorial Garden, VanDusen Botanical Garden and Dr. Sun Yat-Sen Classical Chinese Garden. Additional stops require additional time.

Starting downtown, go south on Burrard Street. After crossing the Burrard Bridge, take a right onto Cornwall St. Follow the marked Scenic Route past Kitsilano, Jericho

Gardens & Parks

Dogwood

British Columbia's official provincial flower is the dogwood. According to the *Chinese Language of Flowers*, the dogwood's virtue is strength and the lesson it teaches is "aversion to evil."

In survey after survey asking why visitors choose to come to Vancouver, gardens are mentioned as one of the top four reasons. The other reasons include its climate and reputed beauty.

A full-colour guidebook, *Gardens of British Columbia* by Pat Kramer, Altitude Publishing, is available in bookstores and gift stores.

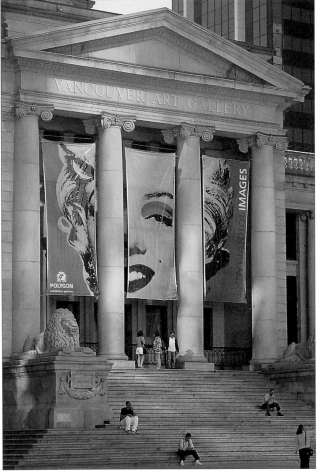

Vancouver Art Gallery

it is particularly notable for its Alpine and Asian research collections. Stop and visit this magnificent 70-acre site if you have the time and energy.

Follow SW Marine Drive to Oak St. and drive north to **VanDusen Botanical Garden,** Vancouver's 55 acre show garden at 5251 Oak Street at 37th Ave., (604) 257-8662 or (604) 878-9274. This garden is a must-see. Allow yourself two hours. Guide-driven electric carts are available for those with limited walking ability. Stop at the on-site **Shaughnessy Restaurant,** (604) 261-0011, for refreshments.

Continue north to **Chinatown** and visit the tranquil one-acre **Dr. Sun Yat-Sen Classical Chinese Garden,** 578 Carrall St., (604) 689-7133, one of the few authentic scholar's gardens outside of China. Guided tours are ongoing.

Strolling Tour 1: Robson Street

Information at (604) 299-9000 ext. 8132.
Start: Robson Public Market, 1610 Robson St. at Cardero.
Finish: BC Place Stadium
Timing: 1.5 hours, not including stops for shopping; best between 9 a.m. and 9 p.m.; good in the evenings too, when the Vancouver "scene" is lively.

Late in the evening, especially on Fridays and weekends, a young crowd walks "Robsonstrasse" under its fluttering banners, just for the sake of walking and being seen. Looking for something specific? Phone the Downtown Vancouver Business Improvement Association, (604) 685-7811.

Robson Public Market,

and Locarno beaches. Stop at **Spanish Banks,** named for early friendly encounters in these waters between British and Spanish naval vessels. Here is a dramatic city view. Continue to the University of British Columbia and stop at the architecturally resplendent **Museum of Anthropology,** 6393 N.W. Marine Drive, (604) 822-3825. Its outdoor one-acre Native Plant Garden features vegetation as it was before contact.

Nitobe Memorial Garden, (604) 822-6038 or for a guided tour, is a 2.5 acre oasis across from the Museum of Anthropology. It is an authentic Japanese stroll and tea garden. A special reduced admission price is available when you combine your visit with the nearby U.B.C. Botanical Garden admission. Periodic formal Japanese tea ceremonies are scheduled from time to time.

Continue past **U.B.C. Botanical Garden,** 16th Avenue and SW Marine Drive, 6804 SW Marine Drive, (604) 822-4208. Established in 1916,

(604) 682-2733, is a fresh food market. A great place to start the pulse of the day, this eclectic street begins with a choice of freshly baked breads and steaming hot coffee.

Silver Blue Traders, 1165 Robson, (604) 737-1444, is one of several souvenir treasure shops with a notable assortment of Native crafts, rhodonite and BC jade.

Starbucks Coffee Co., 100, 1100 Robson or 1099 Robson (604) 685-1099, are two places to order a latté and do a little people watching. Coffee drinking in Vancouver is a must-do.

Murchie's Tea & Coffee Ltd., 970 Robson, (604) 669-0783, a company founded in 1894, packages a wide variety of aromatic coffees and teas and sells British china and porcelain. This store feels like a nostalgic leftover from the old days when Canada enjoyed preferential tariffs with the "mother" country.

Virgin Megastore, Robson and Burrard, (604) 669-2289. An enormous record store first opened in 1996, Virgin Megastore is part of the Richard Branson business empire. The decor is fashioned after his New York store.

Nearby is **Planet Hollywood,** 969 Robson, (604) 688-7827, a popular restaurant owned by Hollywood superstars Sylvester Stallone, Bruce Willis, Demi Moore and Arnold Schwarzenegger. It is filled with props and costumes from many well-known films. Check out the hand prints.

Robson Square, 800 Robson Street between Hornby and Howe, is an architecturally pleasant plaza attached to the Provincial Law Courts

Robson Street

with restaurants and the Robson Square Conference Centre. From time to time, informative public events are held in the Centre.

The Vancouver Art Gallery, 750 Hornby at Robson, (604) 662-4719. Vancouver's ex-courthouse was built in the Neoclassical Revival style and now offers a permanent art collection and revolving art shows. Admission is in the $7 range for adults; Thursday evenings from 5 p.m. to 9 p.m. Admission is by donation.

Pacific Centre Mall, (604) 688-7236 701 Granville St. at

Robson, is an underground complex of 200 stores, boutiques and restaurants. Stop here and you may not emerge for hours.

Three Greenhorns

The "Three Greenhorns" restaurant is named after three luckless gold miners who built their cabin in 1862 near a coal seam at the foot of Bute Street. They went on to claim a huge piece of property encompassing most of Vancouver's West End and most of Robson Street. The cost? $555.75.

Chinatown Gate

BC Place Stadium, Robson at Beatty St., events line (604) 661-7373, was at its

World's Narrowest Building

"Sam Kee" was the name of a business group of Chinese importers who lost a valuable piece of property when the city widened the (now defunct) Dupont Street in 1912. Left with a sliver of land on which they were allowed to build a structure only four feet, eleven inches wide, the infuriated group decided to proceed. The resulting free-standing building is listed in the *Guinness Book of World Records* as the "narrowest building in the world." Upper bay windows extend the usable space on the upper floor to a little under 2 m (5 feet, 10 inches). Communal baths (no longer in use) were built underneath the sidewalk. The narrow building, located at 8 West Pender St., is today abutted against a much wider building, but continues to attract much curiosity.

opening in 1986 the largest air-supported amphitheatre in the world. Up to 60,000 fans can cheer on the BC Lions football team or drop in on home, boat or outdoor mega-trade shows.

Strolling Tour 2: Gastown and Chinatown

Start: The Landing, Gastown, 375 Water St.
Finish: Ten Ren Tea & Ginseng Co., Chinatown, 550 Main Street.
Time: 2 hours, not including shopping; best during daylight hours when the stores and restaurants are open. Chinatown has special nighttime markets Fridays, Saturdays and Sundays from 6:30 p.m. to 11:30 p.m., June through September.

The Landing, 375 Water St.(604) 453-5050, is a mini mall with an impressive arched window overlooking the harbour. It is a good place to stop for afternoon tea. The modern indoor complex contains boutiques and restaurants.

Canadian Impressions, 321

Water St. (604)-646-3900, has a large variety of jewelry, fashions, casual wear, giftware, art prints and native art. Focus is on souvenir and Canadian made goods. Other locations are at #18 Waterford Centre, 200 Burrard St. (604) 646-3935, and 601 Cordova St. (604) 646-3920.

The Inuit Gallery, 345 Water St., (604) 688-7323, is just the right place to discover fine examples of West Coast Native and northern arts. Discover your taste in art.

Hill's Indian Crafts, 165 Water St., (604) 685-4249, features Cowichan sweaters, moccasins and an upper floor (trek up there) of Native screen prints, totems and sculptures. The talking sticks and food bowls are unique; silver jewelry is hand made. To decipher Indian symbols and find more Native attractions, look for two Altitude books: *Totem Poles* and *Native Sites in Western Canada.*

The Gastown Steam Clock, at Water and Cambie streets, was built by horologist or clock maker Ray Saunders. Powered with steam from an underground community heating system, its steam song plays every 15 minutes. Once the only one of its kind in the world, a duplicate was commissioned for Tokyo in 1995. Costumed attendants start free 90-minute guided tours of Gastown from this point or at the Gassy Jack statue; for tour schedules, contact the Gastown Business Improvement Society, (604) 683-5650.

The Fishhead Water Fountain at the intersection of Water and Abbott streets stands near the Lamplighter

Pub in the Dominion Hotel, 210 Abbott St., (604) 681-6666, a heritage property in Victorian Italian style. This Klondike Gold rush period is also known as the T. Roosevelt or Edwardian era. It was the first Vancouver establishment to serve alcohol to women.

Blood Alley, in the lane between Abbott and Carrall streets, and Gaoler's Mews, near the corner of Water and Carrall streets, date from 1850s, when bloody brawls within the former resulted in incarceration in a small unlocked cabin in the latter. Town constable Jonathan Miller ankle-chained the prisoners, who were then guarded by John Clough, a one-armed drunkard. Upon incorporation in 1886, City Treasurer G.F. Baldwin had no source of taxation revenue other than fines levied on town drunks. It is said that he very gingerly counted the well-used, reportedly "odiferous" English sterling and American coin and currency that were collected from over-indulgers.

Maple Tree Square and the **statue of Gassy Jack** on a whiskey barrel marks the intersection of Water, Carroll, Powell and Alexander streets. This was the site of Gassy's second saloon. His first was in New Westminster.

Across the street is **Hotel Europe,** 43 Powell St., (604) 689-5161, a flatiron triangular-shaped building built in 1892 by Italian businessman, Angelo Colari. Known in its day as the finest hotel in town, it was the first fireproof building in western Canada.

R.J. Clarke's Tobacconist, 3 Alexander St., (604) 687-

Gastown's Steam Clock

Positioned on the northwest corner of Cambie and Water streets, the Steam Clock was first unveiled on September 24, 1977. Invented by Roy Saunders, the main whistle on top of the clock is a replica of one that formerly graced the MV *Naramata*, an historic paddlewheeler used to carry passengers and fruit among BC's interior lakeside communities. At the moment of its 20th anniversary in 1997, the heated-vapour clock, faithfully sounding every quarter-hour, had played Westminster Chimes on its steam whistles 438,000 times and in the process entertained about 40 million visitors. No word was released on how often the whistles might have been tuned. "Rarely" would be the best guess.

Weighing in at two tons, the curious clock is powered by excess steam supplied by a somewhat unusual heating company. Rather than building separate facilities, one central boiler system supplies heat to many of the downtown office buildings. Central Heat Distribution Ltd., headquartered at 720 Beatty St., runs six industrial boilers that are 30 feet high and 60 feet long, and maintains more than six miles of underground pipes. It supplies its many clients continuously with an average of 575,000 pounds of steam per hour at 185 pounds of pressure, superheated to 400° F.

4136, was Vancouver's first smoke shop and still is a great place to pick up Cuban cigars.

Continue through a run-down transition zone to Chinatown. Turn right onto Carrall St. and walk three blocks to West Pender St. Start at the corner of Pender and Carrall streets, where in 1911 at the **Chinese Freemasons' Building,** 1 West Pender St., the great Cantonese revolutionary Dr. Sun Yat-Sen took refuge. Here, he organized headquarters for those who helped him

to depose the adolescent Emperor Pu-Yi, who was characterized in the Hollywood movie, *The Last Emperor.*

The Sam Kee Building, 8 West Pender St., is listed in the *Guinness Book of World Records* as the world's narrowest building—2 m (5 feet, 10 inches) in width. Now home to **The Jack Chow Insurance Co.,** this 1913 building once accessed an underground bath house dimly lit by the glass blocks in the sidewalk. **Shanghai Alley,** to the right, was

once a thriving lane but is now in decline.

Walk over to **Canton Alley** on the corner of Pender and Carrall streets. It was once the red light distinct, crammed with opium dens and brothels.

The 1902 **Chinese Times Building,** 1 East Pender St., was home to Chinatown's first newspaper. Many of the neon signs date to the 1940s and the recessed balconies are a traditional feature of the architecture in southern coastal China. Added European details are

"Gassy" Jack Deighton

A broad man with a wicked tongue and a strong arm, "Gassy" Jack Deighton (1830-1875) gave Gastown his colourful name. In 1867, when the cranky curmudgeon first set up shop, "gassy" was a euphemism for a talkative drunkard. Arriving by boat on July 4, fresh from a harsh patriotic dispute with the American co-owner of his saloon in New Westminster, the staunchly British Deighton set to work. Within 24 hours he enlisted carpentry help, built a crude saloon, unfurled the Union Jack, delivered a "blood and guts" speech and thanked everyone with free drinks. After the first Granville survey map came out in 1870, Gassy purchased Lot #1 for $67.50. However, when he subsequently begged Governor Douglas for protection from stabbings and brawls, a customs officer arrived to tax him instead. In

order to keep his liquor license active, he was forced to open an adjoining hotel.

When guests complained about his hotel's basic lack of comforts such as pillows, Gassy and his friends boasted of a plan

to line the streets with rows of troughs, fill them with stinking offal and goo, and trap seagulls for their feathers. As compensation for their rough stay, each overnight guest received a stiff complimentary "eye-opener" before breakfast.

After his first Native wife died, Gassy immediately took up with a second Native woman from the North Shore. When he abused her, she would signal her relatives. They would arrive by boat and remove items of furniture from Gassy's Hotel. Deighton died in the summer heat at age 45. He used his last words to curse a howling dog. Total funeral costs were reported in the daily newspaper at $136.68, including libations. It was a first-class sendoff. To his son, nicknamed the "Earl of Granville," he left $304.89. Gassy's historic saloon/hotel was destroyed in the Great Fire of 1886.

typical of the Sino-Portuguese influences in southeast Asia.

Across the street is **China Gate** and the **Chinese Cultural Centre,** 50 East Pender St. The two chimeras, lion-like figures, are protective symbols. To distinguish male from female, look for the baby. Rotating public displays about the history of Chinatown are displayed in the lobby. Chinese New Year celebrations and others originate here; phone for dates; (604) 658-8865.

Through the courtyard is the must-see **Dr. Sun Yat-Sen Classical Chinese Garden and Park,** (604) 662-3207, at 578 Carrall Street. One of the few authentic Chinese scholar's gardens in North America, it features guided tours, garden shows, displays and evening entertainment. Admission is in the $6 range. Through the round white Moon Gate is the free adjoining park, particularly spectacular in May when the purple Emperor Tree is in bloom. A quick side trip along Keefer St. will take in several of Chinatown's best bakeries. Try one of the goodies.

Back on West Pender St. is the **Wing Sang Building,** 5167 East Pender St. Constructed in the Victorian Italianate style of 1889, it is Chinatown's oldest building and after serving as an opium den, it became home to the first bank to cater directly to the community.

The **Chung Wing Geong Tong Building,** 79 East Pender St., is a "secret" association building created at a time when the community had to care for its own business needs. During the 1920s and 1930s "tong wars" erupted between the tongs or business associations over control of lucrative Asian importing businesses.

The green-balconied **Chinese Benevolent Association,** 108 East Pender St., was established in 1908 to help newcomers overcome discrimination. At that time, most Chinese immigrants were from the province of Canton and

Canadiana Shopping : What to Consider

Looking for a unique gift that is all-Canadian? Try one of these items.

BC arts and crafts: Most easily found on Granville Island, every type of item from jewelry to ceramics is usually well made.

BC ice wines: A new type of wine, it is a definite rage.

BC jade figurines and jewelry: BC's nephrite jade is a waxy green colour.

BC Native art, wood carvings, masks: West Coast Native art is legendary.

BC rhodonite jewelry: Pink rhodonite is sometimes called the "heart" stone.

BC salmon, canned, dried or fresh: Found in many variations from "Indian candy" to deep smoked, it is packed for shipping.

BC silver Native jewelry is made by hand.

BC wines: Originating mostly in the Okanagan Valley, several whites are particularly notable.

Books by Canadian authors: Subjects range from poetry to outdoors.

Canadian beer: With 5 to 6.5 per cent alcohol, it has its loyal fans.

Canadian rye whiskey: A longtime favourite, this aged brew also has its followers.

Canadiana and nature items: All sorts of items from wooden clocks to T-shirts celebrate the beauty of Canada.

Compact disks: Reputedly one of the most economical places in the world to buy CDs, the selection is extensive.

Cowichan knit sweater: Made from sheep's wool, these Native-made sweaters quickly become old favorites.

Cuban cigars: Definitely not Canadian, they are freely available because of Canada's friendly trading regime with Cuba.

Furs: Still a quality Canadian item, Canada mink, lynx, sable, fisher, fox and beaver are fashioned into traditional designs.

Hudson's Bay point blanket: Distinguished by black "point" lines and distinctive colours, these are a lifetime investment to hand down to your children.

Lottery tickets: Anyone from anywhere is entitled to win the lottery and the prizes are paid out in one check. You must claim the prize.

Mountain bikes: Check out the yellow pages. With many quality manufacturers here, the prices are excellent.

Native made moccasins: Made in Brockton, Alberta by the Peigan Nation, these are a comfortable, long-lasting reminder of your holiday.

Outdoor gear and clothing: With all the wilderness around, Canadian gear is best.

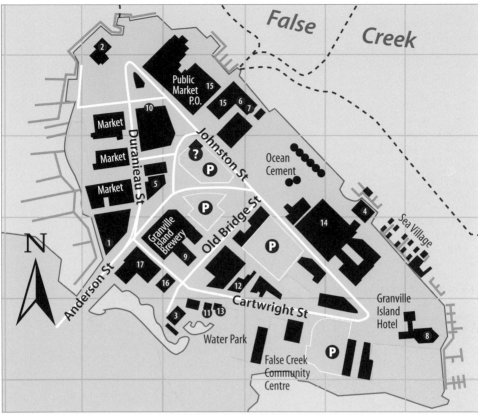

Granville Island Map

Granville Island

Granville Island, once known as Mud Island, is made from dredged and compressed silt collected from the bottom of False Creek.

In 1915, Vancouver's mayor, Mr. Louis Taylor, claimed the Island was created by "nifty patronage and contract padding." Two dredging contracts were drafted: one to dredge a shipping channel, the second to fill an island. The two contracts were combined, effecting a neat profit.

During the Depression until the 1950s, a Shanty town thrived here. The city left the squatters alone. If the people were uprooted, it was decided that they would bloat the city's already overloaded welfare rolls. The shack-dwellers survived by selling firewood, salmon and smelt to locals, and by working occasionally for the industrial concerns located on the island.

In 1973, with $19.5 million in federal capital grants, the facility was rehabilitated. Today the island is owned by the Government of Canada and operated by the Granville Heritage Trust. Over 2,500 people are employed here.

Granville Island

1. The Sirloiner
2. Bridges
3. Isadora's Co-op
4. Joanathan's Seafood House
5. The Keg Restaurant
6. Mulvaney's
7. Creole Café
8. Pelican Bay/Le Bistro
9. Cartwright Gallery
10. Circle Craft Co-op
11. Craft House
12. Potters' Guildk
13. New Leaf Press
14. Emily Carr College of Art & Design
15. Arts Club Theatre
16. Waterfront Theatre, Carousel and New Play Theatre
17. Kids Only Market

are thus Cantonese speakers. Since 1975, most new immigrants have come from Hong Kong and Mandarin-speaking areas. This has resulted in a major readjustment within the community.

The **Won Benevolent Association,** 123 East Pender St., was entirely dedicated to welfare services for families named Won or Wong. Upstairs is a Chinese language school. The predominance of the colour red throughout the area is to encourage vigour and good fortune.

The 1907 **Lee Building,** 127-133 East Pender St., once concealed an opium factory.

Continue past the shops along East Pender to Gore. The 1920 **Kuomintang Building,** 529 Gore St., was once the temporary headquarters for the Chinese Nationalist League, the group that put leader Chaing Kai-shek into power in Taiwan.

Near it, the **New Chong Lung Seafood and Meat Market** at Gore and Keefer streets, is a lively place to see geoduck (pronounced GOOEY duck), salmon and poultry prepared the Chinese way.

The tour doubles back to a well-deserved rest at the **Ten Ren Tea & Ginseng Co. Vancouver Ltd.,** 550 Main Street, (604) 684-1566. This outlet is part of a world-wide operation where you can sample, drink or buy a selection of Chinese teas.

Set aside at least half an hour to peruse **Tung Fong Hung**'s jars, bins and boxes of herbal remedies: whole dried seahorse for menstrual cramps; thin-sliced deer antler for blood loss; bird's nest (up to $500 per 38 grams) for general

Granville Island Public Market

BC Jade

Two minerals fall into the category of jade: jadeite and nephrite. Though chemically and structurally different, they exhibit many of the same characteristics. The Chinese first recognized the difference in 1750; the Europeans in 1863. Nephrite, found in abundance in northern British Columbia around Dease Lake, is prized for its antiquity, carving excellence, and other historical considerations. However, it is the lower-priced of the two types. The colour range of waxy-textured nephrite jade includes creamy white, gray, coal-black and olive green. BC's jade is typically a rich olive green. Jade will shatter; when transporting it, be certain to wrap it well. Ancient peoples, particularly Asian people, believed all jade would ensure a tranquil life and a peaceful afterlife.

intestinal revitalization; and more kinds of ginseng than most people thought existed. Easily one of the most fascinating stores in the Lower Mainland, one of several branches is located at 536 Main St., (604) 688-0883.

Strolling Tour 3: Granville Island

Start: Granville Island Public Market Ferry Dock, 1689 Johnstone St.
Finish: Emily Carr College of Art and Design.
Time: Allow two hours between 9 a.m. and 6 p.m. daily. The recommended time does not allow for shopping. The Public Market is closed Mondays. Arriving by car is a daunting experience, traffic is slow, parking is difficult, cars are towed after three hours without exception.
Mini-ferries: The recommended way to arrive and leave is by foot ferry. Call for information and pick-up locations: Granville Island Ferries Ltd. (604) 684-7781.

The Ferry Dock beside the Public Market is the arrival point for the ferries. Resist the impulse to rush inside the public Market. Look around first.

Locate Mulvaney's, 1455 Johnstone St., (604) 685-6571, is a New Orleans style restaurant.

Best Bets: Distinctive Canadian or BC-made Goods

Dorothy Grant Boutique offers exciting West Coast First Nations designs in ladies' apparel. Timeless pieces such as capes, jackets and vests are available from the Upper Galleria, Sinclair Centre, 1656 W. 75th Ave., (604) 681-0201.

Granville Island features several all-Canadian or all-BC craft and arts outlets.

JAX is clothing label made by women for women in Vancouver from an internationally recognized fashion house lauded for its popular everyday designs. It is located along the Upper Level, Pacific Centre, an underground mall at 701 W. Georgia St. Call (604) 688-7956.

Martha Sturdy Originals is a distinctive outlet for this Vancouver designer's famous jewelry and furniture collections. Found in fine stores and museums, her goods are also sold at 3039 Granville St., (604) 737-0037.

Roots Canada, a home-grown phenomenon since 1973 sells rugged outdoor wear, casual clothing and fun accessories for men, women and children. They have provided Olympic clothing for Canada's and the United States' athletes. Most items are made in Canada. Downtown stores are located at Pacific Centre, an underground mall at 701 W. Georgia St., (604)408-4250; or 1001 Robson St. at Burrard, (604) 683-4305.

Pappas Furs Designers are a third-generation family business selling furs that are often featured in *Vogue* magazine. If you choose, a free limo will take you to visit 449 Hamilton St., (604) 681-6391.

Tilly's Endurables offers well-made adventure clothing for travellers. Featuring durable garments with secret pockets and wrinkle-resistant fabrics, the styles are practical and timeless. Check out the famous Tilly Hat. Located at 2401 Granville at 8th, the phone number is (604) 732-4287. Walls covered in photos and testimonials are part of this fun adventure.

Tony Cavelti is Vancouver's own renowned jewelry designer who handcrafts creations such as engagement rings and gents' pieces in 18k gold and precious stones. His creations are sold at 698 Hastings St., (604) 681-3481.

The Trading Post is located in a restored, rustic 1911 log cabin offering Canadiana, West Coast and Inuit art, knitwear, jewelry and some imports. Located inside the Capilano Suspension Bridge attraction at 3735 Capilano Road, North Vancouver, the phone number is (604) 985-7474.

Zonda Nellis, Canadian designer, internationally recognized for her woven separates, textured sweaters and hand-painted evening wear as well as interior and accessory collections, has one outlet at 2203 Granville Street at 6th Ave., with limited opening hours; call (604) 736-5668.

The Arts Club Theatre, 1585 Johnston St., (604) 687-1644, is right next to the public market. It presents a lively array of plays and musicals; phone for events.

The large **Granville Island Public Market,** 1689 Johnson, 604-666-6655, is the grand-daddy of this former gritty industrial area, now turned squeaky-clean and fashionable. Within its 50,000 square feet is located an ever-tantalizing array of fresh farm and ocean produce as well as in-house bakeries and fast food stops. On the outdoor plaza, jazz musicians, buskers and comedians give sample performances.

The Maritime Market, Duranleau Street from Triangle Square to Anderson St., is the place to buy or sell your yacht, custom build your dream boat, charter a fishing boat, or rent a kayak.

The Granville Island Sport Fishing and Model Ships Museum, 1502 Duranleau, (604) 683-1939, offers model ships, a fly fishing collection, old lures, reels, rods and Roderick Haig-Brown's writings. Admission is in the $2 range.

The Net Loft, 1666 Johnston St., between Duranleau and Johnston, shelters an eclectic array of shops from beads to folk art, paper and glass.

Granville Island Information Centre, (604) 666-5784, has a quick overview of the island's transformation history plus up-to-date information on festivals, shows and performances.

Granville Island Brewing Company, 1441 Cartwright St. on the corner of Anderson and Cartwright, (604) 267-9463, is the place to sample microbrews.

Kids Only Market, 1496 Cartwright St., (604) 689-8447, has 24 toy shops, clowns, and even a day care centre. Next door is a Water Park for kids; ask about changing facilities.

Various galleries along Cartwright St. include potters, glass blowers, artists' galleries and metal sculpture studios.

Granville Island Hotel, 1253 Johnston St., (604) 683-7373, is a good place to stop for a break before walking along the wooden dock to Sea Village, a block of floating homes moored along False Creek.

Emily Carr Institute of Art and Design, 1399 Johnston St., (604) 687-2345, welcomes visitors to its dedicated free-to-view art gallery and main rotunda, where students' works are on display. Return to the ferry dock and catch your ride back.

Best Picks: Shopping Areas

Before choosing an area, check out which kind of shopping you like best from the listings in this book. They include antique shopping, art gallery walks, ethnic neighbourhood shopping areas and First Nations shopping in Gastown or Granville Island.

Gastown along Water Street is an eclectic outdoor area in the oldest part of the city. Now revitalized, the area offers First Nations art, souvenirs, and accessories such as hats. Many restaurants have outdoor patios where people-watching is fun.

Granville Island on Johnston St., (604) 666-5784, is for the arts and crafts buff and features all sorts of local-artist galleries as well as glass blowing studios, food stalls and restaurants. Street entertainment is common. Food is very fresh.

Cuban Cigars

CIGAR ALERT: In August 1997, two U.S. smokers alerted the RCMP to a multi-million-dollar, countrywide explosion in smuggled and counterfeit Cuban cigars. Vancouver was one of the areas that was affected. The two Americans who reported the incident paid a convenience store owner $750 for boxes they believed contained Cohibas, which normally retail for around $1,640 a box. The fakes are often sold in phony boxes, with photocopied rather than embossed labels. Experts can spot the "bumpy" rolling, overly "soft" feel and incorrect degree of "sponginess." Do not buy Cuban cigars from street vendors, corner stores, or unlicensed sources. The outlets mentioned here sell genuine merchandise:

Alpha Tobacco, 829 Denman St., Vancouver, (604) 688-1555, stocks the most exquisite cigars and accessories.

Cigar Connoisseurs, 12 Water Street, Gastown, Vancouver, (604)682-4427, has a walk-in humidor and complete selection.

Havana Land of Cigars, 102 1300 Robson St., Vancouver (604) 602-4747, has a complete selection.

Granville Market

Lonsdale Quay Market on the North Shore at the foot of Lonsdale, has over 80 indoor specialty retail stores, a children's section, a fresh-food market, food stalls and restaurants on the waterfront; call (604)985-6261.

Pacific Centre Mall, Georgia St. and Howe, (604) 688-7236, is a large centrally located underground mall with a maze of over 200 stores and two major department stores. Once you enter, you will be dazzled by its waterfalls and multi-level brand-name stores.

Park Royal Shopping Centre is the North Shore's shiniest shopping centre featuring major department stores on two sides of Marine Drive near Taylor Way. Located at the foot of the Lion's Gate Bridge in West Vancouver, more information is available by calling (604) 925-9576.

Robson Street, considered the fashion pulse of the city, extends to the water from Burrard St. Featuring boutique clothing stores and assorted souvenir shops, the street is open until 9 p.m. most days in the summer. This is also an excellent place to stop for a sip of latté or to go patio-dining; call (604) 669-8132.

Royal Centre Mall, located adjacent to the Hyatt Regency Hotel on the corner of Burrard and West Georgia St., is an underground mall with about 60 stores ranging from souvenir outlets to everyday necessities; call (604) 689-1711.

Sinclair Centre is an indoor mall created from four joined heritage buildings. It houses a small assortment of unusual stores and apparel outlets. Piano recitals in the main foyer are frequent. It is located at 757 West Hastings St.; call (604) 659-1009.

Vancouver Flea Market, with over 360 stalls on a good day, is a five-minute walk from the public transit SkyTrain Main Street Station at 703 Terminal Ave. Eclectic offerings of valuable "junque" are for sale only on Saturdays and Sundays from 9 a.m. to 5 p.m.; call (604) 685-0666.

Waterfront Centre, a small indoor mall, has a few shops, a postal station, and a sheltered plaza with fast food services. Located at the main entrance of Howe and Cordova Streets, more information is available by calling (604) 893-3200.

Yaletown, bordered by Nelson St. on the north and Homer St. on the west, is a revitalized outdoor warehouse area with upscale furniture shops, some youth apparel and eclectic, funky goods as well as several choice eateries. Start walking along Mainland St. in the 1000 blocks.

The Hollow Tree

An icon of Stanley Park, the Hollow Tree has served as the background for thousands of photographs since Vancouver's founding in the late 1800s. Great grandmothers still point to Kodak scenes of happy family outings when the family, in its Sunday best, would take the Model T and drive it inside the cavernous stump. Full-time professional photographers once set up their cumbersome equipment to handle a steady stream of residents and visitors who posed inside it. Countless amateur sports teams and school groups continue to display group photos of happy groups deep inside its dank interior. The Hollow Tree has provided a century of lasting memories to millions of visitors and comforting continuity to generations of Vancouverites.

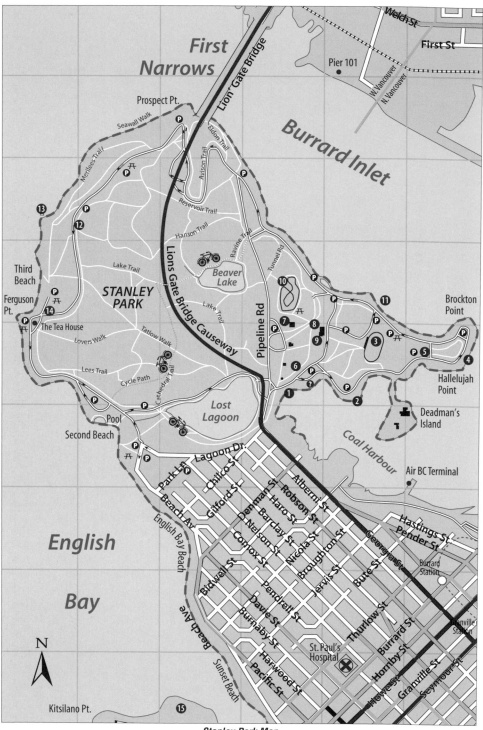

Stanley Park Map

Attractions

1. Vancouver Rowing Club
2. Royal Vancouver Yacht Club
3. Brockton Oval
4. 9 O'Clock Gun
5. Totem Poles
6. Malkin Bowl
7. Children's Zoo
8. Japanese Monument
9. Vancouver Aquarium
10. Minature Railway
11. Girl in a Wet Suit Statue
12. Hollow Tree
13. Siwash Rock
14. Pauline Johnson Memorial
15. Vancouver Museum/Planetarium

Strolling Tour 4: Stanley Park

Though the tour described here is for walkers, those with less time to spare may choose to drive the one-way ring road, Park Drive. Take time to stop at the totem poles and Prospect Point. Parking charges apply 24 hours a day.

If you circle through the park twice, take the left fork upon entering from Georgia St. Then bear right, park and visit the Rose Garden. On your second pass, find the playground, Lord Stanley's statue and the memorial to U.S. President Harding, who died a few days after visiting Vancouver. Children's facilities are steps away.

Start: Lost Lagoon, at the end of Robson Street on Lagoon Drive.

Finish: Lost Lagoon

Time: Allow about three to four hours if you plan to visit the aquarium. On summer Sundays, artists hold a market under the trees. The Seawall Walk around the outside park perimeter is 8.8 km (5.5 miles), but it takes less time on a bicycle or on roller blades. This walking tour covers an interesting section of this huge 1,000 acre park. Bring refreshments; food out-

lets are scarce here.

Lost Lagoon was named by Pauline Johnson, a Mohawk Indian princess who wrote poetry. Before it was separated from the sea, it drained out at low tide and her little pond was "lost." A walk around the perimeter to see its waterfowl is 1.8 km (1.1 miles) in length.

The Nature Centre on the water's edge offers educational displays that describe the park's ecosystem and is the starting points for guided nature walks. Phone for times, (604) 257-8544.

The Vancouver Rowing Club practices on your right, and the Duke of Edinburgh, Queen Elizabeth's husband, is a patron of the Royal Vancouver Yacht Club. On your left is Queen Victoria's Monument. Lord Stanley, governor-general of Canada, opened the

Stanley Park

In 1888, Vancouver's Stanley Park plan was laid out by Frederick Law Olmsted, the renowned designer of New York's Central Park, Brooklyn's Prospect Park, Washington DC's Capitol Grounds, Boston's Park System, Montreal's Park Royale and California's Yosemite National Park.

Lord Stanley, the man who opened the park on October 29, 1889, is better remembered as the person who founded Canadian hockey's championship, the Stanley Cup.

At 440 ha (1,000 acres) in size, Stanley Park is a little larger than New York's Central Park at 340 ha (840 acres).

The 1.7 km Seawall was completed in 1971. A master Italian

stonemason devoted much of his life to building the wall, often standing waist deep in water.

The steep cliffs of Prospect Point are composed of five-sided columns of basalt formed from the solidification of lava 32 million years ago. This geological eruption also led to the formation of Siwash Rock, accessible on foot at the northwestern tip of the park.

There used to be a sign in the park reading "Buffalo left, big trees right."

The first park roads were paved with material found onsite. These were crushed clam shells accumulated from a huge midden near the Salish summer village of Whoi Whoi.

Dead Man's Island earned its name because Coast Salish people used to place their dead high up in trees on this island. Later, it was home to a quarantine hospital for cholera victims.

Nine O'clock Gun, also called "the Time Gun," is a canon fired electrically at 9 p.m. Cast in England in 1816, it was installed in 1894 at Brockton Point, near its present site. In early years, sailing ships relied heavily on tides and accurate time readings. A stick of dynamite was detonated each evening. Ships' officers set their chronometers. The flash, not the noise, was used for the calibrations.

park on October 29, 1889 during Victoria's reign. In the distance is a protruding land mass called Dead Man's Island. Before contact, the Coast Salish people placed their dead high up in its trees.

Hummingbird Trail takes you past Malkin Bowl where you can find washrooms and a small cafeteria. Unless you travel the long Seawall perimeter of the park, this is the only refreshment outlet. Here, you will find Theatre Under the Stars, a summer-only theatre company. A lovely rose garden blooms here in June and July.

Up the path, the **Vancouver Aquarium** is a good way to round out your adventure in this remarkable park. This is Canada's largest aquarium. Its stars are the ever-popular beluga and killer whales. Admission is in the $11.95 range. Call (604) 685-3364.

The Japanese Monument was erected in 1920 as a tribute to honour the 190 Japanese-Canadians who served in World War I. Smaller plaques were added after World War II and the Korean War.

The Vancouver Children's Zoo and **Variety Kids Farmyard** are to your left.

Find the Mallard Trail marker and join Brockton Oval Trail. This cricket pitch is in use some weekends. It is rumored that two bank robbers once buried their ill-gotten gain somewhere in this field. For years, the groundskeepers found mysterious holes in the turf. Head east.

The **totem poles** are an authentic collection of mostly Kwakiutl poles. First gathered from around BC in the 1930s at a time when totem carving

Gardens of Stanley Park

was almost a lost art, the ladies of the Vancouver Museum Society collected poles and commissioned new ones. Only when a great revival of the carving arts occurred during the 1950s did their collection regain the respect it deserves.

An informative book, *Totem Poles* by Pat Kramer is usually available at the **Legends of the Moon** kiosk (604) 408-2181, and explains the totem's symbolism. Totems are family crests or emblems; they were never worshipped.

How Stanley Park Came into Being

A 1,000 acre forested oasis in the midst of a bustling metropolis is an exceptional achievement. More remarkable is the fact that it was during Vancouver's first-ever city council meeting on May 12, 1886 that its brand new aldermen set the park aside. Before we congratulate the city's forefathers on their remarkable insight at a time when trees were the "enemy" and parks were virtually unknown, these revelations may help.

The military strongly supported the area's preservation for strategic purposes. Local lumbermen had already set up a sawmill in today's park area and cut many of its biggest cedars.

Most of the aldermen dabbled in real estate. They estimated that their Gastown properties would devalue if this prime waterfront property flooded the market. Their solution was to create a park. The result: a few lumbermen "against"; military personnel and property owners "for." It passed. When the "park" request reached Ottawa, it was treated with amusement. Due to the intervention of William Cornelius Van Horne, president of the CP Railway, who also dabbled in Gastown properties, the request was eventually granted. It was leased to the City of Vancouver by the federal government in June 1887 for $1 per year.

Kitsilano Beach

Assorted Strolling Tours: Parks and Ocean

Ambleside Beach Park Stroll, 13th and Marine Drive, West Vancouver just north across the Lion's Gate Bridge, offers a beautiful 61-acre waterfront area with beaches, sports facilities, a children's playground, pitch-and-putt golfing along with a picturesque two-mile-long Seawall. Nearby along Marine Drive is **Ambleside & Dundarave**, known as "The Village." Fashionable cafés, boutiques and restaurants attract shoppers while just a stone's throw away, buffed in-line skaters cruise the beach-front Seawall. Pat's Restaurant (604) 926-8922, 445 13th St., a short hop away, serves West Coast cuisine.

Lynn Canyon Park Suspension Bridge Crossing, (604) 981-3103, extension 3366, Park Road, North Vancouver, is a friendly rainforest wilderness complete with a heart-thumping suspension bridge that hangs 50 m (150 feet) above a raging river. Considered a highlight by many, the trails take second place to the exciting, no-charge suspension bridge. There is also a small **Ecology House** with displays for children.

Two of the best Oceanside Strolls are **Kitsilano Beach Park** with the adjoining Vanier Park on Northwest Marine Drive, and the 11 km (7 mile) Stanley Park Seawall. For further information, phone Stanley Park Ecology Society, (604)257-6907.

Pacific Spirit Regional Park Trails on the University of British Columbia Endowment Lands has a Visitor

Cut across to the Seawall on the north side and notice the bright yellow sulphur waiting for export. Over to your right is **Brockton Point,** a lighthouse and navigational aid from the late 1800s. Walk to your left (west) to see *Girl in a Wet Suit,* a statue popular with students who like to dress her in their school T-shirts.

Variety Kids Water Park is a water playground, open on hot summer days only, complete with a miniature railway and periodic pony rides.

From here you can follow the **Seawall** around the park's perimeter; it is about 8 km (5 miles) on foot. Alternately, you can take a cutoff. Check out the accompanying map and head for **Beaver Lake,** a water-lily-covered lake that was once used as the water supply for Stamp's Mill, a temporary sawmill set up before Vancouver's city council took control of the area.

Navigate your way along the trails back to Lost Lagoon. You will undoubtedly pass Weeping Willow Lane, the last part of Stanley Park to be annexed. It was supposed to be Vancouver's first graveyard, but it was so marshy that engineers wisely changed their minds.

Vancouver's Sister Cities

The concept of "sister cities" or "twinning" is the desire to increase and promote academic, artistic, cultural and economic links between cities in different nations. Vancouver has forged official links with Edinburgh, Scotland; Guangzhou, China; Los Angeles, USA; Odessa, Russia; and Yokohama, Japan. Vancouver's sister city relationships began in 1944 with Odessa. In 1985, a 12 member delegation from Guangzhou (Canton) visited Vancouver to sign a sister city agreement. In 1986, Los Angeles City Council voted unanimously to become a twin of Vancouver, and the mayor of Los Angeles visited that June for the signing ceremony.

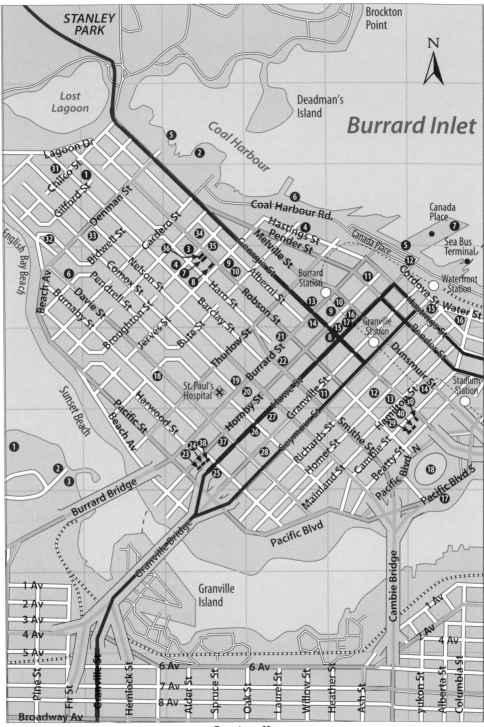

Downtown Map

Centre at 16th Ave. and Blanca St., Vancouver. Stop here for a map of the 50 km (31 miles) of trails set aside for walking or cycling the old-growth cedar forests. At Camosun Bog, find botanical remnants from the last ice age such as arctic starflower and carnivorous sundew. Periodic interpretive tours are available; phone ahead, (604) 224-5739.

Queen Elizabeth Park on Little Mountain, 33rd and Cambie Street, Vancouver, features Quarry Gardens on the 170 m (510 foot) summit. The Bloedel Floral Conservatory, (604) 257-8584, a 23 m (70 foot) dome enclosing three habitats: tropical, rainforest and desert, is also found here. Admission is in the $3.30 range. Next to the dome is a Henry Moore sculpture, *Knife Edge*. Scattered about the 130 hillside acres is an arboretum. Follow signs to the rose garden, Seasons in the Park Restaurant, (604) 874-8008 and a Pitch & Putt golf course (604) 874-8336. Parking fees are in effect.

West Vancouver Centennial Seawall Stroll, Dundarave Pier in the 2400 block, Marine Drive, West Vancouver, features a 2 km (1.2 mile) paved walk along the ocean. From late May through September between 5 p.m. and 7 p.m., cruise ships pass nearby. The Beachhouse at Dundarave Pier, 150 25th Street, (604) 922-1414, serves fine food. Capers Store & Café, 2496 Marine Drive, (604) 925-3374, features fresh fare in an upstairs hideaway.

Strolling Tour 5: Downtown Core

Start: Canada Place, at the foot of Burrard Street.
Finish: Waterfront Station
Time: Allow three to four hours, not including shopping and breaks; recommended for mornings or afternoons.

Canada Place is nicknamed "Under the Sails." A multipurpose facility including a Convention Centre, hotel, restaurant, big screen **IMAX theatre** and World Trade Centre, this complex is also home to a multitude of cruise ships bound for Alaska. With its 27 m (80-foot-high) Teflon™ sails, it is the land-

mark of the harbour. Descriptive plaques around the outside promenade provide entertaining Vancouver histories. Step inside to view the lobbies and totem poles at the Pan-Pacific Hotel and the Japanese influence in the lobby across the street at the Waterfront Centre Hotel. On a rainy day, take in the huge-screen presentation at the CN IMAX Theatre, (604) 682-IMAX. There are three daily shows on the hour starting at noon and two performances in the evening. Admission. Still looking for more information? Pop across the street to the main headquarters of Vancouver's tourist information centre at 200 Burrard Street, (604) 683-2000.

The ornate 1920s art deco **Marine Building** at 355 Burrard Street was once the tallest office building in the British Commonwealth. Costing $2.5 million in its day, its terra cotta friezes depicting Neptune and his creatures are interwoven with bas-relief panels illustrating West Coast history from Spanish galleons to the CPR's great ocean liners. Its com-

Attractions		Hotels			
❶	Vancouver Maritime Museum	❶	Buchan Hotel	㉑	Le Meridien
❷	Vancouver Museum & Planetarium	❷	Westin Bayshore	㉒	Wedgewood Hotel
❸	GM Southam Observatory	❸	Sheraton Landmark	㉓	Executive Inn
❹	Roedde House Museum	❹	Ramada Renaissance	㉔	Quality Inn
❺	Boat Tours	❺	Pan Pacific Hotel	㉕	Vancouver Centre Travel Lodge
❻	Air BC Terminal	❻	Sands Best Western	㉖	Holiday Inn Downtown
❼	CN Imax Theatre/Convention Centre	❼	Barclay Hotel	㉗	Bosman's Motor Hotel
❽	Vancouver Art Gallery	❽	O'Doul's Hotel	㉘	Chateau Granville
❾	Cathedral Place	❾	Pacific Palisades	㉙	Georgian Court Hotel
❿	Canadian Craft Museum	❿	Blue Horizon	㉚	Sandman Inn
⓫	Orpheum Theatre	⓫	Day's Inn Downtown	㉛	Rosellen Suites
⓬	Ford Theatre	⓬	Waterfront Centre Hotel	㉜	Sylvia Hotel
⓭	Vancouver Library	⓭	Hyatt Regency	㉝	Coast Plaza Stanley Park
⓮	Q.E Theatre/Playhouse	⓮	Hotel Vancouver	㉞	Riviera Inn
⓯	Harbour Centre Look Out	⓯	Hotel Georgia	㉟	Greenbrier Hotel
⓰	Gastown Steam Clock	⓰	Metropolitan Hotel	㊱	Robsonstrasse Motor Inn
⓱	Plaza of Nations	⓱	Four Seasons	㊲	Landis Suites
⓲	B.C. Place Stadium	⓲	Parkhill Hotel	㊳	Viva Suites
	and B.C. Sports Hall of Fame	⓳	Century Plaza	㊴	Rosedale on Robson
		⓴	Wall Centre Garden Hotel	㊵	Hotel at the YWCA

mercial elevators once stopped two stories short of the top to ensure the privacy of the penthouse occupants. Albert Cadman, an early superintendent, once fell down an elevator shaft. Upon reaching him, the man sent to dispatch him a glass of brandy drank it himself and fainted. Both men recovered.

Christ Church Cathedral at 690 Burrard, a stone church completed in 1895, was once nicknamed "St. Root Cellar." Financial constraints caused the congregation to stop building for many years after excavating and pouring the basement.

Cathedral Place next door at 925 W. Georgia features a female statue commemorating the sacrifice of nursing sisters during World War I. In the courtyard is the Canadian Craft Museum, 639 Hornby, (604) 687-8266. Admission. On Thursday evenings from 5 p.m. to 9 p.m., admission is by donation.

Hotel Vancouver, 900 West Georgia and Hornby, (604) 684-3131, was completed in 1929 by the Canadian Pacific Railway (CPR) to replace a much earlier "Hotel Vancouver,"—one of a series of distinctive château-style hotels across Canada to promote railway travel. It has elegant copper roofs on which gargoyles are perched, and the lobby is done in a simple Edwardian (T. Roosevelt-era) style. Stop in and have a look at the historic but hilariously inaccurate painting of Captain Vancouver visiting local Natives. At one time, an entire floor was permanently set aside for visiting British royals. When the Prince

Hotel Vancouver

Downtown Vancouver

The Hotel Vancouver once boasted a glassed-in tea garden on the roof, where full orchestra tea dances were held each afternoon. Groups of friends ordered a full afternoon tea and a meal of chicken à la King for 75¢, while budget-minded ladies could order plain crackers and tea for 10¢.

Vancouver has outgrown several nicknames including "City of the Rusty Suntan," "Totemland," and even "Mushroom City." It embraces "The World in a City" or "Gateway to the Pacific Rim," but is unable to shake its designation as laidback "Lotusland."

Vancouver is famous, not for particularly tall buildings, but for "skinny" ones. With astronomical land prices, buildings tend to be narrow. Vancouver's tallest office buildings include: Royal Centre Tower, 1055 West Georgia, and Vancouver Centre, 650 West Georgia, both at 36 stories; Bentall IV, 1055 Dunsmuir, and Park Place, 666 Burrard, both at 35 stories; and the Toronto Dominion Bank, 700 West Georgia St., at a mere 30 stories. Several hotels are much taller.

of Wales stopped by in 1919, the traffic lights at street level were turned off to prevent squealing brakes from disturbing the royal guest. Several midnight car crashes foiled the grand plan.

The Vancouver Art Gallery, 750 Hornby at Robson, (604) 662-4700 was originally completed in 1911 and served until 1979 as the provincial courthouse. Admission; Thursday evenings from 5 p.m. to 9 p.m., admission is by donation. It is closed Monday and Tuesday from October through May. Across the street, the Hotel Georgia is associated with movie actor Errol Flynn. While making arrangements to buy a yacht, he passed away here in a fourth-story room in the early 1950s. The Centennial Fountain in front of the Art Gallery was sculpted in 1967.

Robson Square is across the street from the Art Gallery's Robson St. side, where environmental protesters like to "hang out." The Provincial Law Courts and its slanted glass roof were designed by renowned architect, Arthur Erickson. Continuing along Robson Street is a whole adventure in itself.

Barclay Heritage Square and **Roedde House Museum,** 1415 Barclay St., (604) 684-7040, are historic protected areas. Admission to Roedde House includes a guided tour; hours of operation are limited. The Rattenbury-designed house was built in 1893 by the proprietor of the city's first bookbinding firm. His young son, Bill Roedde, holds the dubious distinction of being the first Vancouver resident to be hit by a chauffeured motorcar. Occurring in 1900, when there were few cars about, the offender was none other than Mr. B.T. Rogers, a local sugar magnate. Rogers had the shaken but uninjured boy driven home in grand style.

Pacific Centre Mall, (604) 688-7236, 701 Granville St., is an underground complex of 200 stores including The Bay, part of the Hudson's Bay Co. chain that was founded in 1637 to trade furs in Canada. There are several food outlets in the shopping mall, and an underground route connects to the **Canadian Venture Exchange,** 609 Granville St. It features a public area for viewing trade transactions. Admission is free. Also in the complex is the Four Seasons Hotel, with its glass-domed atrium and waterfall.

Lookout! Harbour Centre, 555 West Hastings, (604) 689-0421, is well worth the admission of around $8 to travel by

Best Panoramic City Views of Greater Vancouver

The altitude of Vancouver itself averages about 30 m (91 feet) above sea level. The Coastal Mountains across the inlet in North and West Vancouver are clearly the places to go for views. They rise to an average height of 1,220 m (4,000 feet).

Cloud Nine Restaurant, 1400 Robson St., Landmark Hotel, rises 41 stories; (604) 687-0511.

Cypress Bowl Roadside Viewpoint, West Vancouver, Highway 1. Exit "Cypress Park" and travel to the second switchback. Watch for the signs. Parking and picnic tables are available.

Grouse Mountain Skyride travels to the top of a 1,127 m (3,700 foot) mountain. It is located 15 minutes from downtown Vancouver at 6400 Nancy Greene Way, North Vancouver, (604) 984-0661 or (604) 984-7234. Admission is about $17.

Lookout! on top of Harbour Centre, 55 stories, 555 West Hastings St. Vancouver, (604) 689-0421, has helpful signs pointing out 360 degrees of surroundings. Admission is about $8.

Queen Elizabeth Park Outdoor Viewpoint, 33rd and Cambie Street, top of Little Mountain at Quarry Gardens, 140 m (458 feet).

exterior glass-enclosed elevator to the top. Here, an entertaining 15-minute film, historical displays, guides, and a 360 degree view of Vancouver are serviced by a coffee bar—a great place to inspect ships in the harbour.

Waterfront Station, 601 W. Cordova, was formerly the Canadian Pacific Railway Station that represented the completion of Canada's great transcontinental railway from sea to sea. Now the hub for the SkyTrain and Sea Bus, the Victorian-era paintings on the ceiling were created by wives of train engineers.

Lookout! at Harbour Centre

Walking Tours: Public Gardens

Dr. Sun-Yat Sen Classical Chinese Garden, (604) 662-3207, at 578 Carrall Street in Chinatown, is authentically modeled on a courtyard-type scholar's garden. This 15th-century Ming dynasty garden is concentrated into about one acre and because Taoist philosophy is the metaphor for Chinese gardens, its yin and yang features are said to create channels for *ch'i*, a powerful life breath. A guided tour is included; admission is in the $6 range. Phone for information on frequently occurring special events.

Nitobe Memorial Garden, University of British Columbia Campus, across from the Museum of Anthropology, N.W. Marine Drive, is an authentic Japanese garden about 2.5 acres in size, consisting of a stroll garden and a tea garden. Like its kin in Japan, this garden is meant to foster *zanzen*—an enlightened serenity of mind. Admissionapplies, but a discount is in effect if you combine your visit with admission to nearby U.B.C. Botanical Garden. Periodic formal Japanese tea ceremonies are held for an extra charge; phone ahead, (604) 822-6038.

Park and Tilford Garden, (604) 984-8200, is located at #440, 333 Brooksbank Ave., at the southwest corner of the shopping centre, North Vancouver. About 2.5 acres in total, its theme outdoor "garden rooms" include the Native Garden, blue-tiled Moon Gate,

---

Day Trips from Vancouver: Whistler

Now a world-renowned winter ski resort situated in a spectacular glacier-filled mountain setting, Whistler also offers casual summer visitors a variety of outdoor activities, exciting shopping opportunities or gentle trails to explore. The two main mountains, Blackcomb Peak and Whistler Peak, are located side by side and tower majestically above an architecturally controlled village of fascinating tourist shops, outdoor cafes and delicious eateries. The longest ski runs measure a breathtaking 11 km (7 miles) in length and boast a 1.6 km (one mile) vertical drop. State-of-the-art gondola lifts accommodate skiers and snowboarders in winter and serve as summer sightseeing trams to high mountainside restaurants in summer. Whistler's building boom continues unabated and there are always new establishments to discover in a walk around the picturesque but ever-growing villages. Celebrity encounters are commonplace year-round. Check out the patios of the most popular restaurants.

Basics
Whistler resort, with a permanent population of 8,000, is located 123 km (76 miles) from Vancouver on Highway 99.

By private vehicle
Road conditions: (604) 660-9770

By motorcoach
See "Excursion companies" in the listings.

Winter or summer activities
Whistler Activity and Information Centre: (604) 932-2394

Rock Sculptures, East Bay

Asian Garden, White Garden, Rose Garden, Rock Garden, Herb Garden and the Colonnade Garden with a Spanish-style pergola, 70 m (200 feet) in length. Admission is free; there are several coffee houses nearby.

Stanley Park's Flower Gardens at the foot of Georgia Street consist of a rose garden, which is at its best in June and the Ted and Mary Grieg Rhododendron Garden and its magnolias, at its best in May. The one-acre rose garden is near the Stanley Park Pavilion; upon entering the park, take the left fork. The "Grieg Garden," about three acres in size, is near Second Beach; park by the Parks Board Office or nearby at The Tea House, Ferguson Point. Admission to either garden is free; pay parking is always in effect.

U.B.C. Botanical Garden, (604) 822-4208, University of British Columbia Campus, 6804 SW Marine Drive, 16th Avenue and SW Marine Drive, Vancouver, is the oldest university research garden in Canada. Located on a 70-acre site, it includes Asian gardens, food gardens, holly gardens and an extensive alpine garden. Admission, but a discount is in effect if you combine your visit with admission to nearby Nitobe Memorial Garden.

VanDusen Botanical Garden, (604) 878-9274, 5251 Oak St. at 37th Avenue, is the premier garden in Vancouver. Situated on a spectacular 55-acre site, it frequently sponsors special garden exhibit events, so phone ahead. Allow at least two hours to visit this facility's 7,500 plants, two totem poles, two ponds and two lakes. Also open for a Christmas lights display, it is home to Western Canada's largest outdoor garden show in late May. Shaughnessy Restaurant, (604) 261-0011, is open for afternoon goodies as well as meals. Admission.

Day Trips from Vancouver: Victoria

Home to world-famous
The Butchart Gardens, the Empress Hotel, exciting shopping along Government St., international eateries, street entertainment, the Royal British Columbia Museum and the BC Legislative Buildings. For one way travel from Vancouver, allow 1.5 hours for the ferry crossing; one hour or more in the ferry lineups; and a half-hour commute from the ferry terminal to the heart of the city.
Basics
Victoria is a quaint city of 325,000 located on Vancouver Island.
By BC Ferries Schedules and fares: 1-888-223-3779
By sightseeing bus & ferry: See "Excursion companies" in the listings

By scheduled flight:
West Coast Air floatplane service between downtown Vancouver and Victoria., 1061 Coal Harbour Rd. (access from the foot of Burrard St)., (604) 606-6888, rate and schedule info at 299-9000 ext. 6888.
HeliJet Airways daily service between downtown Vancouver and downtown Victoria, 455 Waterfront Rd. (just east of Canada Place) (604) 273-1414 or 299-9000 ext. 1414.
Air Canada has scheduled flights between Vancouver International Airport and Victoria International Airport, 1-888-247-2262
Visitor information & accommodations: Victoria Information Centre, (800) 663-3883 or (250) 953-2033

Culture & Recreation

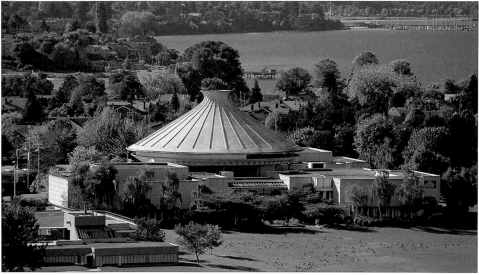

Vancouver Museum

T he many cultures that contribute to Vancouver's arts and recreation scene make it exciting and diverse. Visitors can see aboriginal totem pole carving, Japanese tea ceremonies, music from many European nations, British theatre and a multitude of multi-media art galleries.

History of the Arts in Vancouver

Since the British Navy and the Hudson's Bay Co. first set up a presence on nearby Vancouver Island in the early 1800s, and as soon as Fort Victoria was established in 1842, the earliest BC residents were complimenting themselves on their exceptional flower gardens, leisurely afternoon teas, candlelight dinner dances aboard visiting ships, impromptu amateur plays and other trappings of a "civilized" life. Though visiting officers complained that Victorian ladies' crinolines were behind the 1860s fashions of the time, the elaborate picnics in the country for 45 people, which often included up to 10 wooden cases of food and seven cases of liquor, more than made up for this fashion oversight. Residents sniffed about the "wildness" of the uncivilized American West— and nearby "Granville." New Westminster managed more civility as the home of the navy.

In the 1860s, Vancouver's Granville, now commonly known as "Gastown," was not supporting a naval officer's lifestyle. Its 25 or more saloons were avoided by those of culture. Even the town's only nurse chose to live on the remote North Shore. When medical assistance was needed, saloon keepers hoisted a flag and she rowed across. The Salvation Army soon arrived to rescue Gastown from itself.

However, by the time electricity was introduced to the city in 1887, the first château-style Hotel Vancouver constructed, and the railway link completed in 1889, railroad business managers and politicians began to arrive from the east with definite notions about sophistication. By the spring of 1890, Vancouver residents had enjoyed excerpts from *Carmen* at the new Vancouver Opera House and even the legendary Sarah Bernhardt came to town. Involving themselves in transportation opportunities, the railway barons demanded dining rooms and gentlemen's clubs to augment crude lumbermen's saloons. Several built mansions and a number of splendid parks were set aside for the enjoyment of the citizens. The "ideals of British citizenship" were touted. Victoria's residents breathed a sigh of relief upon visiting the mainland. Grocery selections and fashionable goods appeared in many stores.

By 1900, Count Alvo von Alvensleban, chief ambassador for Prussian Kaiser Wilhelm as well as dozens of European and British aristocrats, arrived in Vancouver to invest, go fishing and shoot game. These long term "visitors" demanded new entertainment including formal dinners, top restaurants, afternoon teas, sporting events, evening plays and musical presentations. The Royal visit of the Duke and Duchess of Cornwall and York in 1901 forced the city to take a major look at itself. "Blueblood Alley" was the name of the socially fashionable residential district (now torn down), and

newly constructed buildings with ornamental facades and historical portraitures soon gave the city a new finesse. By 1911, the Westleyan Moral Reform League forced the Police Commission to vacate the streets of its numerous "madames."

By 1914 there was a marvelous glassed-in tea garden on the top of the Hotel Vancouver and afternoon tea dances were held almost every day. Many indulged in the scalloped chicken à la King at 75 cents, but the economically minded could order crackers and tea for much less. During the Depression, the "Great Gatsby" type of lifestyle enjoyed in the Shaunessy District came to an abrupt halt and it was only in the 1950s that Vancouver once again caught its breath and began to expand its cultural milieu.

In 1959, the Queen Elizabeth Theatre was constructed to host international performances and women who lived in the shadow of their husbands as "patronesses of the arts" sought enduring ways to bestow legacies on the city. An influx of talented young people in the 1960s pushed the arts scene forward and the later

conversion of the old Vancouver Courthouse into the Vancouver Art Gallery proceeded with aplomb. Emily Carr was recognized as the region's most talented historical artist, and recurring celebrations such as the Vancouver Children's Festival entered the scene.

After the city hosted the 1986 World's Fair, Expo '86, a new sense of competence arose among those devoted to the arts scene. Spurred on by a vocal avant garde crowd, a multicultural heritage, cash injections from Canada Council and "Hollywood North," and the profits from sales of arts and crafts, Vancouver's modern arts scene is vibrant and multi-faceted.

Galleries
Gastown Area, Aboriginal and Curiosity Arts Walk

Along Water Street and adjacent Alexander Street there are several interesting galleries featuring First Nations art. Upstairs at

Hill's Indian Crafts, 165 Water St., (604) 685-4249, is a fine selection of West Coast prints and wooden arts. **Inuit Gallery**, 206 Cambie St., (604) 688-7323, sells soapstone and carvings by Northern Inuit artists and masks by the top names in BC aboriginal West Coast art. **Heritage Canada** at 356 Water St., (604) 669-6375, buys First Nations jewelry, carvings and prints directly from the artists (as do other galleries). Antique collectibles and furniture are found a block away at **Bona Wight Antiques**, 72 West Cordova St. along Abbott St. near Water St., (604) 608-1986. **Three Centuries Shop**, 321 Water St. (604) 685-8808, for antiques and fine art; **Salmagundi West**, 321 Cordova St. (604) 681-4648, for quirky, novelty items.

Granville Street, Established Galleries

This walk in Vancouver is one way to take in several established galleries at once. Stroll along South Granville Street between West 6th Ave. and West 15th Ave. **Catriona Jeffries Gallery**, 3149 Granville St., (604) 736-1554, and **Bau-xi Gallery**, 3045 Granville St., (604)733-7011, are long-standing establishment

Notable Art Galleries and Visiting Exhibits

Vancouver Art Gallery, 750 Hornby Street, (604) 662-4719 or (604)662-4700, is Vancouver's premier art-presenting body. Building on a permanent body of works by artists including Emily Carr and an eclectic presentation of contemporary arts, temporary exhibitions draw from all sorts of subject matter from tattoos to centuries of art, drawings, prints, photography, sculpture and paintings. Brief talks relating to current exhibitions take place on Thursdays from 5 p.m. to 9 p.m. and Saturdays and Sundays from noon to 4 p.m. For current information, call (604) 299-9000, extension 5621.
Contemporary Art Gallery, 555 Hamilton St., (604) 681-2700, mounts shiny, slick exhibitions for city dwellers with an urban flare, including pieces about modern directions in architecture.
Diane Farris Gallery, 1565 West 7th Avenue, (604) 737-2629, presents solo exhibitions of new paintings by Vancouver-based artists and others. With striking colours and techniques, this gallery celebrates the beauty of many civilizations.
Helen Pitt Gallery, 882 Homer Street, (604) 681-6740, presents solo installations by feminist, inter-disciplinary artists and others with a message.
Jade World, 1696 West 1st Ave, (604) 733-7212, will allow visitors to watch its artisans at work carving the hard BC nephrite stone. You can view its gallery of fine olive green jade works.
Marion Scott Gallery, 481 Howe St., (604) 685-1934, features high-quality collections of Inuit stone and bone sculptures from talented artists in remote areas of the high Arctic regions; also displays other First Nations pieces.
Morris and Helen Belkin Art Gallery, 1825 Main Mall, University of British Columbia, (604) 822-2759, presents a series of hard-to-predict selections meant to familiarize serious students with the world of art.
Museum of Anthropology, U.B.C. Campus, at 6393 NW Marine Drive, (604)299-9000, extension 3825 or (604) 822-5087. In addition to its permanent collections of aboriginal artifacts and ceramics, it mounts temporary exhibitions of First Nations art. Past exhibits reflecting Northwest Coast artistry have included "Vereinigung," a display of life-sized sculptures of Raven, Wolf and Bear by native artist Connie Sterritt.
Seymour Art Gallery, 4360 Gallant Ave., North Vancouver, (604) 924-1378, is a non-profit community centre highlighting a limited number of high-quality local artist's works. Revolving exhibits change regularly and craft fairs are an interesting addition from time to time.
Vancouver Maritime Museum, 1905 Ogden Ave, (604) 299-9000, extension 2212, or (604) 257-8300, has a permanent collection of art relating to the sea, including painted renditions of great ships and all things marine. Vancouver Museum, 1100 Chestnut Street, (604)299-9000, extension 4431 or (604) 736-4431, sometimes has temporary exhibitions. Past shows have included artifact arts, film, photographs, masks and paintings.
Ferry Building Gallery, Ambleside Landing in the Ferry Building (the ferry is defunct), West Vancouver, (604) 925-7290, is a small facility featuring the artwork of talented North Shore artists.

Burnaby Mountain and Japanese totems

galleries promoting all-Canadian art. **Jennifer Kostiuk Gallery**, 3060 Granville St. (604) 737-3969, features leading contemporary Canadian painters and photographers. **The Art Emporium**, established in 1897, presents major paintings by Canadian, French and American masters at 2928 Granville, (604)738-3510. **Atelier Gallery** at 2421 Granville, (604) 732-3021, once displayed Andy Warhol. **Equinox Gallery** features contemporary painting, sculpture and photography at 2321 Granville St., (604) 736-2405. **Heffel Gallery Ltd.** displays vintage paintings and important art at 2247 Granville St., (604) 732-6505 Contemporary work can be found at **Monte Clark Gallery**, 2339 Granville St. (604) 730-5000. **Uno Langmann Ltd.**, 2117 Granville St. (604) 736-8825, has 18th and 19th century paintings and antiques.

Antique Shops

In several of the city's neighbourhoods, Vancouver's antique shops sell odd assortments of Canadiana, folk art, specialty collectibles, museum quality pieces and case lots from Great Britain's estate sales. Here you might find the odd polar bear rug, a 1940s art deco bedroom suite or an antique kimono.

Antique Row runs along Main Street between East 25th and East 30th avenues. Considered the city's busiest antique district, the stores here are cluttered and very casual, containing old and used "junque" as well as some bona fide "antiques."

Antique Traders are found on South Granville Street between West 7th and West 14th avenues. Carrying high quality collectibles, they also specialize in small pieces of silver, porcelain and jewelry. Uno Langmann Ltd. at 2117 Granville St., (604) 736-8825, specializes in American antique furniture and old paintings. Guild House Antiques is at 2121 Granville St. (604) 739-2141

Canadiana and folk art items are found in the stores along Antique Row listed above, and also in two stores on West 10th and Alma Street.

North Shore antique hunters enjoy treasures displayed at two Lions Mark stores, 1730 Marine Drive, West Vancouver, (604) 926-7710, and 1637 Lonsdale Ave., North Vancouver, (604) 984-6700.

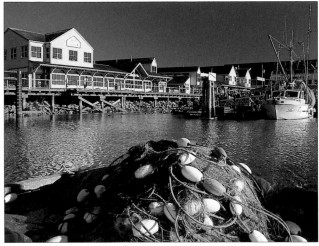

Steveston Village

Granville Island, Arts & Crafts

Stolling in this area is an efficient way to absorb the fun of several galleries at once. **The Gallery of BC Ceramics** 1359 Cartwright, (604) 669-5645, features exotic and colourful works from the bizarre and amusing to the functional and the funky. **Crafthouse Alcove Gallery,** 1386 Cartwright St., (604) 687-7270, goes far beyond amateur crafty pieces, presenting signature glass pieces from the Crafts Association of BC. The annual Regional Show displaying the works of a variety of talented artsy craftspersons is a must-see. Nearby is the **Federation Gallery** with its selection of juried pieces at 1241 Cartwright St., (604) 681-8534. **Creekhouse Gallery** at #3, 1551 Johnston, (604) 681-5016, mounts eclectic displays. Emily Carr Institute of Art and Design includes the **Charles H. Scott Gallery** at 1399 John-

ston St. , (604) 844-3809, as part of the school's familiarization program for its aspiring art students. For works by Emily Carr herself, see the Vancouver Art Gallery. **Malaspina Printmakers Gallery,** 1555 Duranleau Street, (604) 688-1825, is a venerable gallery presenting such works as scrolls or intaglio/woodblock prints by master printmakers. **Eagle Spirit Gallery,** 1803 Maritime Mews (604) 801-5205 for Northwest Coast Native and Inuit Art.

Yaletown Art Walk, the New Generation

Features a series of new galleries cropping up just west of the Cambie Street Bridge along Mainland, Hamilton and Cambie streets. **Dr. Vigari Gallery,** 1839 Commercial Drive, (604) 255-9513, features environmentally friendly art and furniture by local designers. **Coastal Peoples Fine Art Gallery,** #3 1072 Mainland, (604) 685-9298, has a fine selection of aboriginal works.

　　Art Beatus Gallery, M1 888 Nelson St., showcases international art with a focus on contemporary Chinese art.

　　Art Works Gallery, 225 Smithe (604) 688-3301, are renowned for their collection of original canvases, sculptures, monoprints and limited editions.

　　Centre A, 849 Homer St. (604) 683-8326, is the Vancouver Centre for Contemporary Asian Art.

　　Contemporary Art Gallery, 555 Nelson St. (604)681-2700. This new venue for the 28 year old gallery has 6,000 square feet of exhibition, preparation and storage facilities.

Acclaimed Artists from Vancouver

The art world has elevated several Vancouver artists to national and international acclaim. These include: Jack Shadbolt, Bill Reid, Tony Onley, Jeff Wall, Attila Richard Lukacs, Rodney Graham, Zbigniew Kupczynski, Stan Douglas and the venerable Emily Carr.

BC Native Arts

Over the last 10,000 years, the First Nations of the Pacific Northwest Coast gradually developed unique art forms now receiving increased attention throughout the world. Based on defined shapes and concentrating on spiritual figures such as Bear, Wolf, Frog, and Thunderbird, this art has its own special charm. Additionally, native haute couture based on these designs is now coming to the forefront.

A street performer at Granville Island

Haida Creations, 313 Cambie (604) 633-0849, is an active studio where you can see works of native art in progress.

Helen Pitt Gallery, 882 Homer (604) 681-6740, focuses on cultural preservation and development; and stategies of resistance to political, sexist, racial, cultural, individual and economic exploitation and oppression.

Or Gallery Society, 103 480 Smithe (604) 683-7395 has an ongoing commitment to the presentation of comtemporary art that is experimental, challenging and critical, with a priority to Western Canadian artists.

Vancouver Assn. for Photographic Art, 851 Beatty St. (604) 688-6853, is a non-profit society dedicated to furthering the exposure of fine art in the photographic medium.

Vivi Art Gallery, 803 Davie (604) 632-9770, has canvas transfers, custom frames, prints and original artist paintings.

Yale Gallery and Picture Framing, 1230 Hamilton (604)687-6999, features Italian artists.

Performing Arts

Many different types of live drama are presented in Vancouver. Select your favourite. Phone for ticket information: Ticket Master, (604) 280-4444.

Arts Club Theatre, 1585 Johnstone St. on Granville Is-

Arts Hotline

Phone the Arts Hotline at (604) 684-2787 or (604) 684-ARTS. The Talking Yellow Pages Centre Stage has up-to-the minute listings.

Main number: (604) 299-9000
  Arts Club Theatre
    Extension: 8060
  Ballet British Columbia
    Extension: 8057
  Centennial Theatre
    Extension: 8053
  Concert line; rock, country or pop
    Extension: 3080
  Massey Theatre
    Extension: 8054
  Orpheum Theatre

    Extension: 8050
  Queen Elizabeth Theatre
    Extension: 8051
  The Vancouver Playhouse Theatre Company
    Extension: 8059
  Vancouver Opera
    Extension: 8058
  Vancouver Playhouse Theatre
    Extension: 8052
  Vancouver Symphony Orchestra
    Extension: 8056

Totem poles at the Museum of Anthropology

land, (604) 299-9000, extension 8060, or (604) 687-1644, consists of two side-by-side theatres offering entertaining, often award-winning plays from hilarious hit comedy to tragedy at the 480 seat "Mainstage" or the 225 seat licensed "Revue Cabaret." Especially good with cartoonesque satirical works about love veering off the bliss track into wild and uncharted territory, the theatre attracts well-seasoned local and international actors.

Bard-on-the-Beach Shakespeare Festival, (604) 739-0559 or Ticket Master at (604) 280-3311, is a Vancouver original featuring good old bard productions performed in large tents at Vanier Park with a spectacular backdrop of the city, sea and mountains. Summer only from June through September.

Centennial Theatre, 2300 Lonsdale Ave., North Vancouver, (604) 984-4484 or (604) 299-9000, extension 8053. Located on the North Shore, it is a 718-seat functional centre offering a variety of events with an emphasis on travelogue films, Gilbert and Sullivan operettas, children's theatre entertainment and magic shows.

Chan Theatre for the Performing Arts, 6265 Crescent Rd., UBC campus (604) 822-2697 or 299-9000 ext. 8229. The acoustically acclaimed Chan Centre hosts a full range of music , theatre and film events.

Firehall Arts Centre, 280 East Cordova Street, (604) 689-0926, is a small, dark, old building, and hosts top contemporary dance troupes and independent choreographers from Vancouver and around the world.

Frederic Wood Theatre and the U.B.C. Dept. of Theatre at 6354 Crescent Road, (604) 822-2678, present to-

gether a series of plays from time to time. Past presentations have included "Moliere's Shorts," an evening of three one-act plays by the 17th century French playright illustrating that nothing much has changed, least of all folly.

Orpheum Theatre, Granville St., (604) 665-3050 or (604) 299-9000, extension 8050, is a grand old dame, handcrafted and lovingly restored once again from its first incarnation as a cinema in 1926. Once the largest theatre in Canada with its 2,700 seats, this lavish chandelier hall is home to the Vancouver Symphony Orchestra and hosts a variety of other entertaining big name events. For the story of the theatre itself, phone (604) 299-9000, extension 8067.

Queen Elizabeth Theatre Hamilton at Georgia, (604) 665-3050 or (604) 299-9000, extension 8051, still wears its 1959 style well. It is a 3,000 seat venue for major headliners, symphonies, operas and celebrity performances. Home of the Vancouver Opera and Ballet British Columbia, its 70-foot-wide stage is Vancouver's multi-purpose venue for Broadway shows, pop and rock concerts, opera and dance, as well as live broadcast gala award ceremonies and telethons.

Theatre Under the Stars, (604) 687-0174, features family entertainment in a scenic open-air setting among the tall cedar trees in Malkin Bowl in Stanley Park, mid-July to mid-August only. It usually presents upbeat Broadway-style musicals on misty summer evenings.

Vancouver East Cultural Centre, 1895 Venables & Victoria St., (604) 254-9578, is a rustic, creaky old playhouse where Vancouver presents the latest in international theatre, dance or music.

Vancouver Playhouse Theatre Company, located within the Queen Elizabeth Theatre on Hamilton at Georgia St., (604) 873-3311 or (604) 299-9000, extension 8059, stages six or more productions each season including classical or contemporary drama as well as dance, comedy, musicals, recitals and Canadian plays. It is home to Friends of Chamber Music and the Vancouver Recital Society.

Vancouver Theatresports League at the Arts Club Theatre, New Revue Stage, 1585 Johnson St., Granville Island, (604) 687-1644. World champions perform comedy improvisation with help from audience members who supply situations, characters or

Granville Island Comedy Fest

themes

Waterfront Theatre at 1410 Cartwright Street, Granville Island, (604) 685-6217, is home to the Carousel Theatre, (604) 669-3410. It offers outstanding children's theatre and other fairly light-hearted productions with amusing themes such as "couch potatoes meet manifest destiny."

Museums and Planetariums
Major Museums
Always check opening hours and admission rates.

The BC Sports Hall of Fame and Museum, BC Place Stadium, Gate 5, 777 Pacific Blvd. South, (604)687-5520, covers BC sports heroes past and present. Displays include tributes to BC's wheelchair athlete Rick Hansen and hero Terry Fox. For older kids, there are exercise machines, rowing machines and a place to calculate the speed of your baseball throw.

The Canadian Craft Museum Cathedral Place Courtyard at 639 Hornby St., across from the Hotel Vancouver, (604) 687-8266, mounts outstanding professional displays of useful arts by first-rate craftspeople.

H.R. MacMillan Planetarium and Pacific Space Centre, 1100 Chestnut Street, (604) 299-9000, extension 3214, or

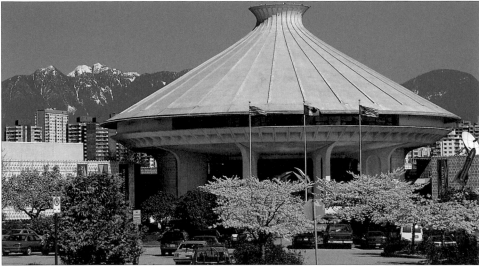

Vancouver Museum

(604) 738-STAR, presents the sun, moon, stars, asteroids and comets along with periodic guest speakers such as BC's first astronaut Dr. Robert Thirsk, a member of the Columbia Shuttle mission STS-78 in July 1996. Admission varies with the program.

Museum of Anthropology, U.B.C. Campus, 6393 NW Marine Drive, (604) 299-9000, extension 3825, or (604) 822-3825, presents changing exhibits and a permanent collection related primarily to First Peoples and secondarily to other aboriginal cultures around the world.

Vancouver Aquarium Marine Science Centre, Stanley Park, (604)299-9000, extension 3210, or (604) 659-3400, in addition to its live fish, whale and reptile exhibits, has periodic shows on such subjects as remote control submersibles, the deep sea and other marine themes.

Vancouver Maritime Museum, 1905 Ogden St., (604) 299-9000, extension 2212, or (604) 257-8300, features a large outdoor totem pole whose twin was presented to Queen Elizabeth II. It presents changing exhibits such as "Shipwreck" or "Airplane Disasters" and permanent exhibits of marine art and artifacts as well as tours of the RCMP's St. Roch, the first vessel to navigate the legendary Northwest Passage twice.

Vancouver Museum, 1100 Chestnut St., (604) 299-9000, extension 4431, or (604) 736-4431, is identified by its giant crab fountain. Beautiful Vanier Park is the backdrop for displays on the city's history, past settlement and present life along with a glimpse at the future of urban life and the Pacific Rim.

Best Bets: Special Interest Museums

Many of these museums are staffed by volunteers; a small admission fee is charged. Donations are much appreciated. Visitors seeking encounters with Vancouver locals are encouraged to visit with the interesting people who keep these places alive. Be warned: always phone ahead to establish hours of operation. These museums may close without notice.

An observatory telescope for the public is located at U.B.C. It is open from time to time on clear nights; please call ahead for hours of operation; call (604) 822-6186.

B.C. Golf Museum, 2545 Blanca St. (604)222-4653, is dedicated to the preservation and promotion of golf history in British Columbia.

Gordon Macmillan Southam Observatory and telescope for the public at 1100 Chestnut Street, near HR Macmillan Planetarium, (604) 738-2855. Phone ahead on clear nights to check if it is open.

Granville Island Model Ships, Model Trains and Sport Fishing Museums, 1502 Duranleau, (604) 683-1939, features model ships, a fly fishing collection, old lures, reels, rods and conservationist Rod-

Library Square

erick Haig-Brown's writings.

Hastings Mill Store Museum, 1575 Alma Street, (604) 734-1212, is the only building known to have survived Vancouver's Great Fire in 1886. Full of bits and pieces recalling Vancouver's pioneering past, the main beam of the store is a piece of awesome timber made from a single log.

Herbarium Museum, Biological Sciences Building at the University of British Columbia, (604) 822-3344, showcases some of the plant-based items now arousing intense interest in healing circles.

Holocaust Education Centre, #50 - 950 W 41st Ave, (604) 264-0499, has periodic exhibitions including a past presentation entitled "On the Edge of the Abyss: Drawings as Eyewitness Testimonies," an exhibit of 93 drawings by Holocaust survivor Ella Liebermann-Shiber.

Japanese Canadian National Museum, #120-6688 Southoaks Cres., Burnaby (604) 777-8000, is located at the Nikkei Heritage Centre.

Museum of the Exotic World, 3571 Main St., (604) 876-8713, features displays from large beetles and insects to stuffed crocodiles and photographs of cannibals. This museum-of-the-strange is a hit with kids who like to "gross their parents out" and anyone who likes the unusual.

North Shore Museum and Archives, 209 West 4th Street, North Vancouver, (604) 987-5618, features simple displays of Coast Salish artifacts, ongoing regional community displays, a diorama and a collection of 9,000 black and white historical photographs. The museum is open Wednesday to Sunday from noon to 5 p.m.

Pacific Mineral Museum, 848 West Hastings St.(604) 689-

8700, presents the art and science of minerals in terms that relate to how they fit into our daily lives.

Presentation House at 333 Chesterfield Ave, North Vancouver, (604) 986-1351, has photography displays of modern, international and historical interest. Past special presentations have included "Rights and Realities," a photographic journey across Thailand, Gaza, Eritrea, Canada, Peru and the Ukraine by six Canadian female photojournalists.

Roedde House Museum, 1415 Barclay, (604) 684-7040, is a restored heritage house serving tea during its limited opening hours. Guided tours are available.

Spencer Entomological Museum, Department of Zoology, University of British Columbia, (604) 822-2211 or (604) 822-2131, has dozens of mounted insects and butterflies.

Vancouver Police Centennial Museum, 240 E. Cordova, (604) 665-3346, is touted as the #1 police museum in North America. It has some bizarre and unusual displays on the hilarious history of crime including a weapons display, counterfeit currency and a coroner's forensic exhibit.

Vancouver Wax Museum, 314 Water St., beside the Steam Clock (604) 683-5813, displays famous people in history, past and present; includes a chamber of horrors.

West Vancouver Museum and Archives, 680 17th St., West Vancouver, (604)925-7295, has a small collection of artifacts and photographs relating to the settlement of West Vancouver and the building of the Lions Gate Bridge.

Literary Arts

Vancouver Public Library—Main, 350 West Georgia Street, (604) 331-3602, sponsors author readings and other gala literary events. Past presentations have included the "City Poets Series" with readings by Canadian poet Margo Button. The library itself is an architectural wonder that merits a closer look; guided tours are available periodically.

Classical Music, Opera and Ballet

Current happenings and celebration festival information is recorded at (604) 684-ARTS.

Ballet British Columbia, (604) 299-9000, extension 8057, or (604) 732-5003, often works with visiting companies of international renown to mount productions under the dance Alive! series. These include both innovative works and enchanting classics. Performance season is from October through April.

Christ Church Cathedral, 690 Burrard Street, (604) 682-3848, is the venue for a free series of presentations of Gregorian chant and medieval polyvocal compositions every Sunday at 9:30 p.m. This is a rare chance to hear twelfth-century music within the superb acoustics of a Cathedral.

Vancouver Cantata Singers, (604) 280-3311, use the Orpheum Theatre, corner of Smithe and Seymour, as their venue to present a series of concerts each season. Past works have included J.S. Bach's "The Passion According to St. John" with James Fankhauser conducting the Pacific Baroque Orchestra and prominent guest soloists.

Vancouver Opera, at home in the Queen Elizabeth Theatre, West Georgia at Hamilton Street, (604) 299-9000, extension 8058, or (604) 683-0222, presents at least one major opera each season. Past presentations have included a multi-media interpretation of Puccini's final work, "Turandot," the story of a Sphinx-like Chinese princess who beheads all suitors who are unable to answer her three riddles.

The Vancouver Symphony, at home in Queen Elizabeth Theatre, located on Hamilton at Georgia, (604) 299-9000, extension 8056, or the Vancouver Symphony Hotline at (604) 876-3434, is a travelling company. They do performances in inspirational venues all over the Lower Mainland. Past performances have taken placc on the mountains at Whistler and at Shakespearean festivals, and the ensemble has often taken its audiences on voyages to the stars.

The Vancouver Recital Society sponsors periodic performances by international artists at various venues. A charge-by-phone service is available at (604) 280-3311; current information is available at (604) 602-0363. See page 39 for the Vancouver Chamber Music Festival.

The Entertainment and Music Scene

Concerts: For current information, call (604) 299-9000, extension 3080.

Two Popular Literary Festivals

Sunshine Coast Festival of the Written Arts is an all-Canadian writers' festival with a very strong following, held near Vancouver for three days early each August. First-time novelists, young adult fiction writers, famous novelists, travel saga story tellers, cookbook authors and naturalists bring excellent entertainment to participants who attend lectures in a verdant garden. Information is available at (604) 885-9631 or (800) 565-9631.

Vancouver International Writers Festival takes place on Granville Island and features readings, international and Canadian authors' visits and vibrant discussions in late October for five days. Information on this dynamic event is available at (604) 681-6330.

Events for teens: For current information, call (604) 299-9000, extension 4812.

Festivals and events: For current information, call (604) 299-9000, extension 3232.

Jazz and rhythm: For current information, call the Jazz Hotline, (604) 872-5200.

Movie show times, Vancouver: For current information, call (604) 299-9000, extension 3106.

Rock and pop, country and folk: For current information, call (604) 299-9000, extension 3080.

Sports and fitness: For current information, call (604) 299-9000, extension 3040.

Symphony Hotline: For current information, call (604) 876-3434.

Best Bets: Jazz, Blues and Fusion

Barclay Lounge, 1348 Robson St., (604) 688-8850, presents various styles.

Blue Note Jazz Bistro, 2340 W. 4th Ave., (604)733-0330, offers a middle-of-the-road jazz favourites.

Capones Restaurant and Live Jazz Club, 1141 Hamilton St. (604) 684-7900.

Cascades Lounge (Pan Pacific Hotel) 300-900 Canada Place (604) 662-8111.

Cellar Jazz Café, 3611 Broadway W. (604) 738-1959 for a laid back evening of primarily jazz with a bit of funk, soul and R & B

Chameleon Urban Lounge, 801 W. Georgia St., (604) 669-0806, is an often-crowded space that nonetheless features good jazz. At least Harry Connick Jr. thought so one night, when he gave an impromptu performance here.

Coastal Jazz & Blues Society, (604) 872-5200, is the contact number for locating year-round concerts featuring jazz, blues, world and improvised music in a variety of concert halls & nightclubs, as well as information on the annual DuMaurier International Jazz Festival.

DV8, 515 Davie St., (604) 682-4388, is a funky new haunt with a decidedly nouveau-bohemian atmosphere and local avant-garde art. It presents tarot card readings on Friday nights. Jazz in an acid vein is featured occasionally.

Fairview Pub, 898 West Broadway, (604) 872-1262, presents the best of rhythm and blues every night of the week such as Jack Lavin or Sunday Jam; live bands play from 9:45 p.m.

Hot Jazz Club, 2120 Main St., (604) 873-4131, is an endless source of emotional jazz excitement. Phone for the latest listings.

Jupiter Café, 1216 Bute (604) 609-6665.

Marquee Grill, 911 Denman St. (604) 689-1181.

Monk McQueen's, 601 Stamps Landing (604) 877-1351.

Railway Club, 579 Dun-

smuir St. (604) 681-1625, offers a broad range of music styles

Rossini's (Kits) 1525 Yew St. (604) 738-7465 and **Rossini's (Gastown),** 162 Water St. (604) 408-1300.

St. Andrew's Wesley Church, 1012 Nelson Street, (604) 683-4574, presents renditions of Rev. John Gensel's original "Jazz Vespers" in which Vancouver jazz artists gather every Sunday to tie their music in with the story of the Bible.

Starfish Room, 1055 Homer Street, (604) 682-4171, presents Coastal Jazz and Blues, French jazz guitar wizards playing in the tradition of Django Reinhardt and gypsy-inspired jazz.

Sugar Refinery, 1115 Granville St. (604) 683-2004 has a laid back atmosphere with good vegan food.

The Purple Onion Jazz Cabaret, 2nd Floor, 15 Water Street in Gastown, (604) 602-9442, presents live jazz, blues and funk seven nights a week plus a nightclub featuring recorded music and dancing.

Gaming Establishments

Casinos and Bingo Halls:
Grand Casino, 725 South East Marine Drive, (604) 321-4402
Great Canadian Casino, 709 West Broadway, (604) 872-5543
Great Canadian Casino, 1133 W. Hastings St., (604) 682-8415
Royal Diamond Casinos Ltd., 106B - 750 Pacific Blvd. South, (604) 685-2340; recorded

information at 299-9000, extension 8111
Planet Bingo features fully electronic bingo permitting big prizes playing on paper or computer screens, 2655 Main St., (604) 879-8930
Gateway Casino, 611 Main St., (604) 688-9412

False Creek, Granville Island

Best Bets: Vancouver Night Clubs & After Hours Entertainment

A quick call to these clubs will confirm entertainment headliners and club specialties.

Aztec Club, 364 Water St., (604) 685-2212.

Babalu's, 654 Nelson St. (604) 605-4343; recorded info: 299-9000, ext. 4343.

Balthazar Lounge/ Hideaway, 1215 Bidwell St. (604) 689-8822.

Brandi's Show Lounge, 595 Hornby St. (604) 684-2000.

The Brickyard, 315 Carrall St. (604) 685-3978.

Club 23 West, 23 West Cordova in Gastown (604) 662-3277.

Daddyo's on Broadway, 1236 West Broadway, (604) 733-2220.

Palladium Corp., 1250 Richards St., (604) 688-2648.

Kits on Broadway, 1424 W. Broadway St., (604)736-5811.

Lotus Club, 455 Abbott St., (604) 685 7777, a women's bar.

The Wett Bar, 1320 Richards St., (604) 662-7707; recorded information: 299-9000, extension 6277.

Richard's on Richards, 1036 Richards Street, (604) 687-6794; recorded information: 299-9000, extension 6794.

Roxy Nightclub, 932 Granville St., (604) 331-7999; recorded information: 299-9000, extension 7699.

Shark Club Bar & Grill, 180 W. Georgia St., (604) 687-4275.

Starfish Room, 1055 Homer St., (604) 682-4171.

Stone Temple Cabaret, 1082 Granville St., (604) 488-1333.

The Rage, 750 Pacific Blvd. South, (604) 685-5585; recorded information: 299-9000, extension 5585.

Railway Club, 579 Dunsmuir St. (604) 681-1625

The Raven Neighbourhood Pub, 1052 Deep Cove Road, North Vancouver, (604) 929-3834; recorded information: 299-9000, extension 2111.

Town Pump, 66 Water St. in Gastown, (604) 683-6695; recorded information: 299-9000, extension 8696.

The Side Door Cabaret, 2291 West Broadway (604) 733-2821.

Wild Coyote Bar and Grill, 1312 SW Marine Dr. (604) 264-7625.

Yale Pub, 1300 Granville, (604) 681-9253.

Yuk Yuk's Comedy Club. 750 Pacific Blvd. (604) 687-5233; recorded info: 299-9000 ext. 5233.

Best Bets: Spirited Fun

A fun way to meet locals is to have a pint or two, watch a televised sports game, or drop in at a local watering hole.

Here is a cross section of centrally located places with a description of the atmosphere so you can choose the setting that suits you best.

Bacchus Lounge in the Wedgewood Hotel, 845 Hornby St., Vancouver, (604) 689-7777, falls into the "upscale comfort" category by providing you with a cosy easy chair and a view of the courthouse. After a few Bacchus martinis, it may be possible to strike up a conversation with a few of the legal or business regulars who make this a convivial place.

Backstage Lounge Patio, 1405 Anderson St., Granville Island, (604) 602-9595, is worth a stop for the view alone; the skyline of False Creek looms over marinas and crowds. The influence of the adjacent Arts Club is evident and the best conversations are about the state of the arts.

Barclay Hotel Pub 1348 Robson St., (604) 688-8850, falls into the "Quiet Urban Oasis" category and is well located half a block west of the tourist promenade on Robson Street. In a nondescript Edwardian building, the peaceful lounge is home to a white baby grand and the regulars who play it.

Billy Bishop Branch No. 176, **The Royal Canadian Legion,** 1407 Laburnum St., in Kitsilano, (604) 738-4142, falls into the "private-club-you-can-get-into-if-you-really-want-to" category. Members freely welcome any drop-in visitor who expresses an interest in military history. Examine the hundreds of plaques from Canadian, Commonwealth and Allied units lining the walls or join in a sing-along of wartime favourite, "We'll Meet Again, Don't Know Where, Don't Know When."

Diva at the Met, 645 Howe Street, (604) 602-7788, in the Metropolitan Hotel, falls into the "upscale comfort" category. It is a sleek bar overlooking Howe Street—Vancouver's (pardon the comparison) equivalent of Wall Street. You can consult your favourite Vancouver stockbroker, who may well be in residence from time to time.

Dover Arms, 961 Denman St., (604) 683-1929, falls into the popular "ye olde pub" category. It is the kind of establishment portrayed in English literature—a crowded, cheery place with a Cockney landlord, darts by the fire and warm ale. With "luckless" Andy Capp cartoons scattered about and Hunky Bill's (Ukranian) fast food chain serving perogies rather than mushy peas, the Canadian beer is your best bet there.

Gerard in the Sutton Place Hotel, 845 Burrard St., (604) 682-5511, falls into the "upscale comfort" category and is

Diana Krall: Mellow Sounds

Pianist-singer Diana Krall is a rising star whether singing or playing…or both! Hailing from the island town of Nanaimo, BC, Diana recalls her grandmother's house and the whole family playing the piano and singing on Sundays. Though she first studied classical piano, it was jazz in the school band with bass teacher Bryan Stovell that resulted in Diana's first gig at age fifteen in a Nanaimo restaurant. She's been playing ever since and after a meteoric rise, she ended up being the darling of the Manhattan night scene.

Diana studied on a Vancouver Jazz Festival scholarship at Berklee College of Music in Boston and met Jeff Hamilton and Ray Brown when they performed in the Pacific Northwest. They encouraged Diana to venture to Los Angeles and there, a Canadian Arts Council grant enabled her to study with pianist Jimmy Rowles. He became her musical "grandpa." Hamilton's musical partner, bassist John Clayton, befriended Diana and they often performed together as a trio. Hamilton and Clayton are featured on one of Diana's early albums, "Stepping Out."

In 1984, Diana settled in Toronto, where she studied with bassist-pianist Don Thompson. She arrived in New York in 1990, but she continued to perform in Boston with a trio that included bassist Whit Browne and drummer Klaus Suonsaari. Diana admires a bevy of great piano players and singers including Nat King Cole. "He could turn his body and sing incredible songs to his audience, and at the same time play unbelievable piano! It was like he was two persons performing at the same time. I hope that one day I will be able to discover the secret of doing this naturally."

Among Diana's achievements are Grammy winner for Best Jazz Vocal Performance 2000 and Juno Award winner for Best Jazz Vocal Album 2000. Diana's latest album is "The Look of Love".

False Creek Walkway

sometimes the bar of choice for the cast of the current movie-of-the-week set. There are few feelings as refreshing as sinking into the leather chairs here. Except for paparazzi, the atmosphere is that of an exclusive London club. The icy martinis are works of art. Lineups are common at this film-industry hangout.

King's Head Creative Food & Beverage Co. 1618 Yew St., (604) 733-3933, falls into the "ye olde pub" category with

the compelling summertime sunny-day bonus of a fine outdoor patio overlooking Yew Street and the nearby Kits Beach. The resulting parade scientifically illustrates what the (sadly) rare combination of good genes, healthy living and youth can do for a body.

Malone's pubs and restaurants in two locations: 2202 Cornwall, (604) 737-7777, and 608 West Pender St., (604) 684-9977, fall into the "Big TVs" category and the atmos-

phere at both locations is decidedly reminiscent of the long-running 1990s sitcom, Cheers.

Pan Pacific Hotel Lounge, 999 Canada Place, (604) 662-8111, falls into the "upscale comfort" category and delivers a classic ocean-and-city view from the licenced area. It improves during the summer, when the adjacent outside deck is open. A Pacific Breeze Martini is a perfect accompaniment for watching the sun-

duMaurier International Jazz Festival

For the last week and a half of June, Vancouver incorporates jazz and blues into its downtown routine. Outdoor shows take place in Gastown and on Granville Island as well as in downtown shopping areas, while the poshest venue, the Orpheum Theatre, welcomes old and new visiting jazz legends.

Past performers have included Bill Frisell, a creative guitarist working in avant garde realms of

jazz and rock crossovers; Cyrus Chestnut, a hot young pianist who cut his teeth as a sideman with Roy Hargrove, Wynton Marsalis and Betty Carter; and Madeleine Peyroux, already garnering acclaim for her blend of jazz, blues and soul.

The event includes a two-day New orleans-style street festival held in historic Gastown. Among the 1400 musicians who took the

stage for the 2001 festival were John Pizzarelli, Metalwood, John Scofield, Clarence Gatemouth Brown and Chris Potter.

A booklet lists the free outdoor shows as well as ticket performances. Telephone 800-GET JAZZ, or (604) 872-5200.

set and enjoying the entertainment of the current pianist.

Panama Jack's, 1180 Howe St., (604) 682-5225, falls into the "quiet urban oasis" category for those who like a bright atmosphere, walls of glass and a high ceiling. The idea is to join in a game of Scrabble or Yahtzee.

Park Royal Hotel Pub, 540 Clyde Ave., West Vancouver, is just yards away from the Lion's Gate bridge, (604) 926-5511. It falls into the smallish "ye olde pub" category with its Tudor and stucco finish, and is nestled in a grove of trees and gardens beside the Capilano River. A crackling fireplace and wood paneling create a pleasant atmosphere for clientele who enjoy one of the better pub lunches in town.

Railway Club, 579 Dunsmuir St., (604) 681-1625, falls into the "private-club-you-can-get-into-if-you-really-want-to" category. A small annual fee gets you into a comfortable atmosphere featuring some of the best original music in town, with a reduced cover charge for members.

Rose & Thorne, 755 Richards St., (604) 683-6467, falls into "ye olde pub" category, so you might want to order a pint of Bateman's Bitters. The main seating area is divided into oversized snugs and you may well find yourself surrounded by grips and gaffers as Hollywood North movie crews (not stars) drop in.

Squarerigger Neighbourhood Pub, 1425 Marine Drive, West Vancouver; (604) 926-3811, falls into "ye olde pub" category, decorated as it is with distracting bits and pieces of nautical ornamenta-

A busy Gastown street

tion. It is a good place to replenish you energy after a stroll along Ambleside Beach.

Sylvia Hotel's Bar, 1154 Gilford St., (604) 681-9321, falls into the "great view" category. In the 1950s, this quiet but legendary little room was the place "hip" mothers used to counsel their daughters on how to be grown-up and safe in Vancouver. Picture windows look out over English Bay for interesting people-watching views.

The Flying Beaver, 4760 Inglis Dr., Richmond, (604) 273-0278, is popular for its location, not in the downtown but adjacent to a sea-plane terminal

Vancouver Comedy Clubs

Comedy is simply a funny way of being serious. Check for show times and headliners.

Lafflines Comedy Club, 26 - 4th Street, New Westminster, (604) 525-2262.

Vancouver Theatresports League, 104-1177 West Broadway, (604) 738-7013.

Yuk Yuk's Vancouver, 750 Pacific Boulevard. South, (604) 687-5233, has great stand-up comedy and a full dinner menu. Recorded information: (604) 299-9000, extension 5233.

quite near the main airport. "great view" is its category and besides the assurance that there is always something with engines to watch, the contemporary lodge-style room is easy on the eyes and the pub grub is a cut above the norm.

Maverick's on the Waterfront, Plaza of Nations, 770 Pacific Blvd. South, (604) 683-4436, is a restaurant and pub that falls into the "ye olde pub" category. Its periodic toe-tapping music is always fun and it has a "with it" ambiance on those hot summer evenings when a festival is held onsite. It is owned by members of the Irish Rovers, an Irish singing group (often pronounced the "Irish Rosers" as the evening progresses). During Expo '86, this place was so popular, the servers had a contract with Brinks Security to pick up their tips twice a day. Ask for a local "brewski." Recorded information is available by calling 299-9000, extension 4436.

Yale Hotel Beer Parlour, 1300 Granville St., (604) 681-9253, falls into the "music-overcomes-the-decor" category. It is an old-fashioned, run-down beer parlour in a seedy area where those low down blues go well with (quite) a few pints. Cover charges apply when itinerant blues man Roy Rogers or Clarence "Gatemouth" Brown come a calling.

Best Bets: What's Open Really Late?

For a city that seems to be having a serious love affair with strong coffee, it is amazing how the tenor of Vancouver slows perceptively at the stroke of midnight. Perhaps the people of Lotus Land are not really sleeping, they are just meditating until morning light. There are a few hives of activity and service if you know where to look. Be advised that as in all large cities, late night security and personal safety in Vancouver are increasing problems.

Benny's Bagels, 2505 W. Broadway, (604) 731-9730, is a people-watching place that serves bagels. Open 24 hours on Friday and Saturday. See also The Naam Restaurant.

Blue Boy Town & Country Bowl & Billiards, 745 S.E. Marine Drive, (604) 325-2695, features billiards and bowling alleys, open from noon to 2 a.m.; and public bowling from 11 p.m. to 2 a.m.

Bread Garden, 2996 Granville St. (604) 736-6465; 24-hour salads, pasta, baked goods, sweets and coffee.

Calhoun's Bakery Café, 3035 W. Broadway, (604) 737-7062, 24-hour sandwiches, salads and standard fare.

Crystell & Cristophir, (604) 683-2061, 9 a.m. to 12 a.m., psychic readings by phone.

Darby D. Dawes Cold Beer & Wine Shoppe, 2001 MacDonald St., (604) 731-8750, 11 a.m. to 11 p.m., beer and wine to go.

Dial-A-Law, (604) 687-4680, provides 24-hour service through the British Columbia chapter of the Canadian Bar Association for practical information on a variety of legal topics. Check the Yellow Pages for lawyers on call 24 hours.

Pumpjack Pub, 1167 Davie St., (604) 685-3417, Friday to Saturday, noon to 1 a.m.

DV8, 515 Davie St., (604) 682-4388, Saturday and Sunday, 5 p.m. to 4 a.m., Monday to Friday, 5 p.m. to 3 a.m., European-style café.

Fairview Beer and Wine, 888 W. Broadway, (604) 708-2337, 10 a.m. to 11 p.m., beer and wine.

Fresgo Inn Restaurant & Bakery, 1138 Davie St., (604) 689-1332, 8 a.m. to 3 a.m., popular cafeteria-style eatery.

Granville Book Co., 850 Granville St., (604) 687-2213, Friday to Saturday, 9:30 a.m. to 1 a.m., Sunday, noon to midnight, Monday to Thursday, 9:30 a.m. to 12 a.m., books and magazines.

Hamburger Mary's, 1202 Davie St., (604) 687-1293, Sunday to Thursday, 7 a.m. to 3

Two Good Bets for Sports Fans

Courtnall's Sport's Grill, 118 Robson (604) 683-7060

A sport fan with a thirst would do well to head to the Courtnall's Sports Grill, a restaurant co-owned by former Vancouver Canuck Geoff Courtnall. It dispenses beer and sports broadcasts in a wholesome atmosphere, and is the third best place to spot Canucks.

Shark Club, Sandman Inn, 180 West Georgia (604) 687-4275

The "video thing" seems to work for the Shark Club, judging from the lineups of people trying to get in. This is one of the city's most popular singles bars and the second best place to spot members of the Canucks having an after-game brew. The first is at GM Place, the "Garage."

a.m., Friday and Saturday, 7 a.m. to 4 a.m., diner-style gay hangout.

Kinko's, 1900 W. Broadway, (604) 734-2679 and 789 Pender St. (604) 685-3338, 24-hour photocopying, desktop publishing, laminating, binding and passport photos.

Martini's Restaurant, 151 W. Broadway, (604) 873-0021, Saturday, 3 p.m. to 3 a.m., pizza, vegetarian and Greek dishes.

Money Mart, 1195 Davie St., (604) 606-9555, 24-hour cheque cashing, wire transfers, money orders, money services.

Pharmacy, open late or all night, **Shoppers Drug Mart,** 1) 885 West Broadway, (604) 708-1135; 2) 2302 W. 4th Ave. (604) 738-3138; 3) 1125 Davie St. (604)669-2424. Several other pharmacies are open until midnight. Consult the Telus Yellow pages under "Pharmacies."

Renegade Productions, 402 Pender St., (604) 685-0435, 24-hour album reproduction, concert production, rehearsal studios.

Robin's Donuts, 1985 E. Hastings St., (604) 251-9566, open until 2 a.m.

Senor Pepperoni's Gourmet Pizza Co., 2184 Cornwall Ave. (604) 739-6999. Gourmet pizza, pasta and salads right across from Kits Beach.

Silver Coin Laundromat Ltd., 2822 W. 4th Ave., (604) 734-9943, 7 a.m. to midnight, laundromat services.

Spargo's Seafood and Pasta House, 1796 Nanaimo St., (604) 253-5525, Friday 11:30 a.m. to 4 a.m., Saturday 4 p.m. to 4 a.m., Greek and Italian food.

Granville Square

Planet Bingo, 2655 Main St., (604) 879-8930,11 a.m. to 12 a.m., bingo hall.

The Naam Restaurant, 2724 W. 4th Ave., (604) 738-7151, 24-hour vegetarian menu and people-watching.

Vineyard Restaurant, 2296 W. 4th Ave., (604) 733-2420, 24-hour standard fare

plus good Greek food.

Wong Kee, 105 E. Broadway, (604) 873-1711, Tuesday to Sunday, 11 a.m. to 3 a.m., late-night chow mein.

Wonton Noodles, 1991 E. Hastings St., (604) 253-8418, 11 a.m. to 3 a.m.; and 4008 Cambie St. (604) 877-1253, Chinese-style noodle house.

What's Happening in Sports?

Vancouver sports fans support a number of professional and amateur leagues ranging from the NHL's Vancouver Canucks to the CFL's Lions. For updates on the latest happenings or ticket information, consult the following phone service.

Talking Yellow Pages Sports: (604) 299-9000

National sports scores updates	Extension: 3050
Vancouver Canucks NHL hockey	Extension: 3055
NHL Hockey report	Extension: 3056
Vancouver Canadians baseball	Extension: 2255
Vancouver Whitecaps soccer	Extension: 8666
BC Lions CFL football	Extension: 3355
Fraser Downs Horse Racing	Extension: 7223

BC Place Stadium

Professional Sports

NHL Hockey: Vancouver Canucks

The Vancouver Canucks' NHL hockey action takes place from September through May at the Canucks' home in General Motors Place. For up-to-the-minute information, contact the Talking Yellow Pages, (604) 299-9000, extension 3055 or the recording at the Events Hotline, (604) 899-7444. Tickets are available through Ticketmaster Charge-By-Phone, (604) 280-4444 or at Gate 10, General Motors Place, 800 Griffiths Way, Vancouver.

CFL Football: BC Lions

The CFL football season kicks off with pre-season games in June and powers through the regular season from July through late October. The Lions were the 2000 Grey Cup Champions. The playoffs and Grey Cup are held in November. For information on Lions games, call (604) 589-ROAR or (604) 299-9000 ext. 3355. The CFL Pro Football report is available at (604) 299-9000, ext. 3041. The NFL Football report is available at (604) 299-9000, ext. 3049.

Vancouver's Professional Car Racing Scene

Billed as the "world's fastest street party," the fastest weekend of the year speeds to Vancouver for three days around Labour Day in September. At this time, the Molson Indy series celebrates another great year of racing at the PPG CART World Series at Concord Pacific Place. Some of the world's top drivers, including greats such as Michael Andretti, Alex Zenardi, Christian Fittipaldi, Jimmy Vasser, Paul Tracy and Dario Franchetti come to town to compete. In past years, Greg Moore, British Columbia's homegrown success story also starred. In addition to the race, the Molson Indy MotorSport Expo is held at BC Place Stadium. At the time of this writing, some residents are trying to halt this racing event, claiming that it interrupts their peace and quiet. However, City Councillors have approved the race event up to 2004. Check it out at (604) 682-4639.

Action on Wheels

For general information on bicycle dealers, call 299-9000, extension 9729.

Bicycle Rentals

Spokes Bicycle Rental and Espresso, 1798 West Georgia St., (604) 688-5141

Bayshore Rentals, 745 Denman St., (604) 688-2453

Bike Races

The following races are held for amateurs during the months of July and August. For further information, call Cycling BC, (604) 737-3034. For entry fees (if any) and times, please contact the numbers listed. Watching the races is usually free.

Canada Cup National mountain bike tour makes a stop in Whistler with cross-country and downhill.

Gastown Grand Prix, (604) 737-3034, is held on July 1.

U.B.C. Criterium, (604) 228-2278, is a road race in Vancouver.

Pedal Down the Peak. Velo-City Cycle Tours Inc., (604) 924-0288, presents West Coaster Mountain Bike Tours down Grouse Mountain. Modeled after Hawaii's volcano bike tours, the experience is not a mad dash down the mountain but rather, a gravity-assisted guided tour with plenty of stops and a bite to eat. Safety is the first priority.

Bicycle Paths

Vancouver Seaside Bicycle Route, constructed in 1990, is a continuous 15 km route from Stanley Park along the north shore of False Creek to Spanish Banks. For a copy of the bicycle route map, contact: Engineering Department, 8th Floor, City Hall, 453 West 12th Ave., Vancouver, BC, V5Y 1V4; (604) 873-7323.

The Greater Vancouver Regional District publishes a road map to guide bicycle commuters safely through the Lower Mainland's streets. It shows both road and trail routes and includes safety tips, rules of the road and directions on how to use bridges, tunnels and ferries. The map also has a colour-coded network to rank the suitability of roads and trails for cycling. The map provides commuter cyclists with some expert advice on how to travel across the region, using both the road system and the growing number of bicycle-oriented facilities. For a copy, contact the Greater Vancouver Regional District, 4330 Kingsway, Burnaby, BC, V5H 4G8; (604) 432-6200.

In certain cases, BC Transit will allow bicycles aboard their

Vancouver Canucks Make NHL Hockey History

On February 11, 1982, NHL history was made when referee Kerry Fraser awarded the Canucks two penalty shots in the same period. Thomas Gradin and Ivan Hlinka both made good on their opportunities against Detroit goaltender Gilles Gilbert. Hlinka's shot was executed with 30 seconds remaining in the third period and gave the Canucks a 4-4 tie.

In 1994, the Canucks came within a one-goal heartbeat of winning the Stanley Cup against the New York Rangers in the seventh game of the finals and in July 1997, Vancouver was abuzz with the $20 million three-year contract signing of veteran superstar Mark Messier. It was said to be a miracle that a top performer like Messier could be lured back into a Canadian team's ranks, but his leadership nonetheless provided the team with a notable advantage. Mike Keenan as coach adds a determined, winning dimension to team morale.

The Canucks' 1997 logo (some say it looks like a demented whale on speed) is called "Shockwave" and follows on the heels of earlier, unforgettable uniforms like the black and orange "Halloween witches" seasons, when Tiger Williams and Darcy Roda were the big names. Still holding a proud record for most career penalty minutes, the ever-colourful Tiger and other hockey legends get together for "old-timers games" and other exciting spectator events.

public transit vehicles. Some, like the West Coast Express, have special bicycle racks. For information, contact Public Transit Customer Information, (604) 521-0400; or (604) 299-9000, extension 2233.

Action on the Run

The following races are held for amateurs during the months of July and August. For entry fees (if any) and timing, please contact the numbers listed. Watching the races is usually free. For general information on fitness centres, call (604) 299-9000 ext. 3040.

Du Worlds Qualifier Duathlon, (604) 250-0614, in Langley.

Locarno Beach Triathlon & Duathlon, (604) 738-5008 or The Running Room, 879-9721, a 5 km swim, 40 km ride, 10 km run in Vancouver.

Knee-knackering North Shore Trail Run, (604) 988-0694, is Canada's most famous ultramarathon: 50 km along the North Shore's Baden-Powell Trail

SRI Chinmoy 12 km Trail Run, (604) 439-9656, one loop around Burnaby Lake on woodchip trails.

Vancouver Half Iron Triathlon, (604) 876-4443 or 800-343-4466, a 2 km swim, 90

BC Lions Football

With 55,097 fans in attendance, the BC Lions last won the classic Grey Cup championship in 1994 with a last-second field goal to steal it away from Baltimore. However, with the gloss of that Grey Cup win behind them, plus heavy competition for market share from the CFL's Vancouver Canucks and the new NBA Grizzlies, the BC Lions and the CFL in general are said to be losing their luster.

However, all is not lost. It is worth noting that British Columbia-grown Pamela Lee Anderson, Baywatch beauty and wife of Motley Crue drummer Tommy Lee, got her big break when Labatt's plucked her from obscurity at a BC Lions football game in 1989. *The Globe and Mail* recently crowned Pamela "the undisputed Queen of the Internet" when it was discovered that she was the focus of no less than 7,000 Web sites, placing her far ahead of the runner-up, supermodel Cindy Crawford. That is one kind of BC Lions winner!

Back in 1909, Earl Grey, the governor-general of Canada, donated a trophy for the Rugby Football Championship of Canada. The trophy, subsequently known as The Grey Cup, was originally open to competition only for teams registered within the Canada Rugby Union. Since 1954, only teams within the Canadian Football League (CFL) have vied for the Grey Cup. Many years ago, in the days of outdoor-only stadiums, the Grey Cup was held in Vancouver every second year. With the mildest climate in Canada, it was hoped that the weather for the late November game would be bearable for more fans. With the advent of modern covered stadiums, the Grey Cup now takes place in one of several Canadian venues.

Spectator Sports Venues in Vancouver

General Motors Place, Gate 10, General Motors Place, 800 Griffiths Way, also called "The Garage," is administered by Orca Bay Sports and Entertainment group. It is the scene of a number of sports and entertainment headliners ranging from championship skater Elvis Stoiko to Canucks NHL Hockey and magic illusionists like David Copperfield. Nominated by US Performance magazine as Area of the Year, it won first place, beating out Madison Square Gardens, NY; Palace of Auburn Hills, Michigan; and US Air Arena, Maryland. The nomination was based on diversity, quality of show, staff and marketing expertise. For up-to-the-minute information on what is happening, listen to the recording at the Events Hotline, (604) 899-7444. Tickets are available through Ticket Master charge-by-phone, (604) 280-4444.

BC Place Stadium, Gate H, 777 Pacific Boulevard South, administrated by BC Pavilion Corporation, is also host to spectator events and sports happenings from rock concerts and monster truck rallies to BC Lions CFL football. For up-to-the-minute information, listen to the appropriate recording at the Events Line, (604) 299-9000 ext. 3215. Tickets are available through Ticket Master Charge-by-Phone, (604) 280-4444.

km cycle, 20 km run, plus a 10-90-10 duathlon from Jericho Beach.

Mountain Express-Leukemia Run, 4/10km, Mount Seymour (604)733-2873.

Coho Salmon Run, North Vancouver (604) 988-0901.

Delta Half Marathon, (604) 597-0403, early registration required, sponsored by The Running Room.

Crescent Beach Triathlon, (604) 250-0614, Olympic length tri in South Surrey.

Beat Bay-thoven Classic, 3, 5, 10 km, White Rock (604) 531-1410.

Summerfast, 5 and 10 km, (604) 684-3560, an evening race on the U.B.C. campus.

Whistler Summer Triathlon & Duathlon, (604) 876-4443 or 800-343-4466, Olympic-length tri and 5-40-5 duathlon course.

Run for the Ferry, (604) 947-9601, a 5 and 10 km run or walk on Bowen Island.

Ironman Canada, Penticton (250) 490-8787, i the only sanctioned Ironman race in Canada, with a 4 km swim, 180 km ride and a 42 km run.

Terry Fox Run, many locations: Fred Fox (604) 464-2666.

Women's 8K Run or Walk, Vancouver (604) 736-6107, for all women of all fitness levels; 4km walk open to men and women.

The Bigfoot Half Ironman Triathlon and Duathlon, Official Qualifier for the World Endurance Triathlon. Harrison Hot Springs, (604) 876-4443. Triathlon: swim 2km, bike 90km, run 21km. Duathlon: run 8km, bike 90km, run 21km.

The CANUSA Triathlon Championship, Harrison Hot Springs 1-800-343-4466. Swim 2.4 miles, bike 112 miles, run 26.2 miles.

Canadian Fall Duathlon, (604) 876-4443 or 800-343-4466, 5 km run, 30 km cycle, 5 km run in North Vancouver's Seymour Demo Forest.

World Endurance Duathlon, (604) 876-4443 or (800) 343-4466, a 13-mile run, 112-mile cycle and 13-mile run in Langley.

Professional IndyCar Driver: Greg Moore

Born in 1975, professional race car driver Greg Moore was brought up in Maple Ridge, BC on the outskirts of Vancouver. Having won five Indy car races, Greg was killed in a crash in 1999 at age 24. Greg's career saw a mercuric rise through several championship auto racing teams, his contract with Player's Forsythe Racing Team, and his Reynard-Mercedes seat.

Beginning on go-karts in 1986, Moore won the North American Enduro Kart Racing Championship and by 1992, he was the USAC Formula 2000 West Rookie of the Year. In 1994, at 18 years old, he became the youngest driver ever to win an IndyCar-sanctioned event with an IndyLights victory at the season opener at Phoenix. Earning a total of three victories and two pole positions, he finished as and the youngest competitor ever in the series.

By his third year of serious competition in the 1995 PPG-Firestone Indy Lights Championship, the 20-year-old won the driver's title in the ninth race of the season at Cleveland. Driving a Player's Lola Buick GS, Moore broke Canadian Paul Tracy's 1990 record with five consecutive wins, scored a seventh pole of the season, and after a string of victories, won his 10th race in the season's finale at Laguna Seca.

By 1996, his purse was $789,750 on the strength of seven top-seven finishes for the PGG CART World Series—including three podium appearances. By March 1997 he finished fourth behind Michael Andretti in the season opener, then went on a few days later to his first IndyCar win of the season in Milwaukee.

In 1998 Greg won in Rio de janeiro and took the U.S. 500 at Michigan. He won the season-opener at Homestead Miami Speedway and led the championship after the first three races. In 1999 he signed a three-year contract to drive for Roger Penske in 2000-2002.

Greg attributed his motivation to his father, and says the best advice he received was: "Always give 100 per cent." He admired the drive to succeed in others and said that waiting in line drives him crazy. His advice to young drivers is never to give up, and he admitted that the worst part of his job was losing.

He is remembered for his winning spirit and gracious deportment. The Greg Moore Golf Classic tournament to raise money for charities was started by Greg and has been sponsored annually by his father, rick Moore and his wife, Donna.

Cycling through Pacific Spirit Park

Action on Water

The British Columbia coast-line offers some of the most ecologically diverse areas in the world. The abundant assortment of wildlife includes whales, seals, sea lions, birds, bears and a more. For general information on boat charters, call 299-9000, extension 9778.

Ecomarine Ocean Kayak Centre, 1668 Duranleau St. on Granville Island, (604) 689-7575, reminds visitors that coastal kayaking is an activity for people of all ages and lifestyles. Kayakers enjoy ocean waters, lakes and slow-moving rivers, or the tranquillity of a protected bay. Misty islets and sheltered channels, home of the Coast Salish people, form a natural environment rich in indigenous history. Local tidal action creates a coastal wilderness teeming with life and ideal for paddling. The area provides habitats for many species including bald eagles, porpoises, river otters, orcas and sea lions. Sea arches and caves are sculpted by the ocean's timeless ebb and flow, while beaches meet the water's edge.

Deep Cove Canoe and Kayak Rental, Deep Cove on the North Shore, (604) 929-2268.

Awesome Wilderness adventures, 214-5683 Hampton Place, Vancouver (604) 736-2147. Provides quality scheduled and custom Eco-Adventure tours in Howe Sound, Squamish, Sunshine Coast and more.

Ayla Canoes rentals and sales, Pitt Lake (604) 941-2822, provides access to Widgeon Creek.

BC Sports Hall of Fame

In 1954, at the British Empire Games in Vancouver, British athlete Roger Bannister and Australian runner John Landry both broke four minutes in the legendary "Miracle Mile". Bannister had recently been the first human to ever break the four-minute barrier, and narrowly beat out Landy for the gold.

This and many other record-breaking events are recalled at the colourful BC Sports Hall of Fame and Museum in BC Place Stadium, Gate 5, 777 Pacific Blvd. South, or (604) 687-5520. Displays include tributes to BC's wheelchair athlete Rick Hansen and hero Terry Fox. For those who get restless viewing the displays, there are exercise machines, rowing machines, and a place to calculate the speed of your baseball throw.

Motor Racing Memorabilia in Vancouver

• For motor racing products and accessories, see Red Zone Motor Sports, 280 East 7th Ave. (604) 707-0507.

• For licensed motor sports collectibles and a large selection of F1, Indy and Nascar products, authentic team clothing, videos or die casts, visit Power Motor-sports, 781 Denman St. at Robson, (604) 608-0848.

• Wilkinson's Automobilia sells collectibles, miniatures, books and automotive art. Drop into 2531 Ontario near Broadway, (604) 873-6242.

Running along the Seawall in Stanley Park

Bowen Island Sea kayaking, Bowen Island (604) 947-9266. Features three hour tours, sunset and full moon paddles and island tours.

Boundary Bay Water Sports. 1-15531 24 Ave., White Rock (604)541-9191. Canoe and sea kayak tours to Indian Arm, Crescent Beach, Semiahmoo bay and Burrard Inlet.

Buntzen Lake Rentals, 3295 Sunnyside, Anmore (604) 469-9928.

Captain Holidays Kayak and Adventure School at Whistler (Vancouver number: 604-905-2925), instructional courses, kids and family programs, river tours and guiding.

Due West Charters, 647 Ewen, New Westminster (604) 524-6031, offers kayak tours, nature cruises and specialty cruises.

Sea Kayak Association of BC (604) 290-9653.

Natural West Coast Adventures, 1308 Everall St., White Rock (604) 535-7985, features tours which focus on observation of the natural marine and wildlife indigenous to the Coastal Region. Watch for grey whales, sea lions, harbour seals and ocean dwelling bird life. Call for kayak tours rentals and instructions.

Ocean West Expeditions, 1750 Beach, Vancouver (604) 688-5770, sea kayak expeditions to Johnstone Strait, Cape Caution, gulf Island and Desolation Sound.

Vancouver Nature Adventures, 1-800-528-3531 or (604) 684-4922, provides wilderness day trips for softies including canoeing, kayaking, and motor cruises. Whale watching, Aboriginal canoe paddle, family canoe rides and river paddling also offered.

Water Challenges and Races

The Alcan Canadian International Dragon Boat Festival, (604) 688-2382, takes place in and around False Creek for three days in the second half of June. With teams from many countries, 100 local teams and 2500 paddlers, this colourful festival has been going strong since 1986.Races include both competitive and recreational categories. Steeped in Chinese tradition, it has become a multicultural water sport and food event. Top entertainment also accompanies the races, with international food dishes, craft exhibits and activities such as an interactive adventure for all ages located inside Enterprise hall and The Plaza of Nations.

Pulling Water Canoe Sports Challenge, (604) 952-2060, July or August. Mixed relay: women paddle from Ambleside to Whytecliff

Park in West Vancouver, men paddle back, 15 km each way, part of the Pacific Challenge series.

Canoe Racing BC (604) 460-0584, is the Provincial Sport Governing body for Sprint Canoe and Kayak in British Columbia. Members include competitive athletes, developing athletes, enthusiasts, coaches, officials, administrators and supporters of the sport.

Ross Wins Snowboarding's First Olympic Gold

In February of 1998 at the Nagano Olympics in Japan, snowboarder Ross Rebagliati won the sport's first-ever Olympic gold medal by ripping down the hill at an insane speed. But this Vancouver/Whistler resident's daring run was soon to pale next to the course he steered through a series of post-race controversies. In the space of 24

hours, he went from hero to zero, and then soared into the category of international phenomenon. First, he tested positive for trace amounts of marijuana, about 18 nanograms or 18 parts per billion. The typical measurement for a single puff is 400 nanograms. Maintaining his extreme cool, Ross denied smoking, but guessed that he had inhaled some smoke from his send-off party. The International Olympic Committee and the Canadian Ski Federation

The History of the Half Pipe

Vancouver's snowboarding scene is active and there are several hills where boarders rage. The roots of snowboarding's half-pipe extend back to the West Coast phenomenon of ocean surfing in the 1950s and 1960s. By 1975, California's skateboarders, seeking greater thrills, had progressed from flat downhill streets to the flowing curves of drainage ditches. Increasingly, they flocked to skateboard parks, where clever designers fashioned wave formations out of rippling cement bowls. Eventually, they experimented with snow bowls.

Throughout the 1970s, most U.S. and Canadian ski resorts dismissed snowboarding's potential and refused to allow snowboarders on their slopes. A handful of diehards sought out winter's frozen creek beds and drainage ditches. Snowboarding pioneers Mark Anolik, Bob Klein, Allen Arnbrister and Terry Kidwell began to use a spot in a city dump they named the "Tahoe City Pipe." To make the pipe rideable took a lot of shoveling. "We spent more time shaping than riding. It wasn't

really about air, " explains Bob Klein. Over the next few years, pro skateboarders Mike Chantry, Rob Roskopp, Steve Cabellero and Scott Foss visited. Photographers from *Thrasher* and *International Snowboard* magazines were close behind—not for the amateur one-hit pipe, but because of the celebrity skateboarder visits.

Then Keith Kimmel appeared on the cover of the first issue of *Absolutely Radical* riding the "Tahoe City Pipe." Everyone in the newly evolving sport began to look for naturally occurring quarterpipes. A chunky halfpipe was constructed for the first Snowboarding World Championships in 1983 in Soda Springs, CA. Tom Sims explains, "They built the pipe, but it wasn't very good. I was extremely disappointed. Then the Burton Team threatened to boycott the contest because they felt halfpipe riding had nothing to do with snowboarding." It was a West-East battle. The western Sims riders had been riding the pipes, while the eastern Burton riders were downhill racing. The West won.

Over the next few years, pipes improved and riders began to boost some real air. By 1986, the World Championships moved to Breckenridge, CO and despite some problems, snowboarding began to take off. Since 1990, halfpipes have been definite media magnets and "big airs" are big news. U.S. and Canadian resorts gradually realized that well-built halfpipes attracted people to the sport.

Today's pipe builders use surveying equipment and mechanical Pipe Dragons (specially modified Snow Cats) to groom the walls. Pipes hundreds of feet long are built to exact dimensions as published in the "International Snowboard Federation Rule Book." Riders say they love to ride halfpipes—if ski resorts build good ones.

British Columbia's ski resorts agree. Snowboarders are pampered, not only with half pipes, but with a variety of special features called fun parks or terrain parks. These include pipes, table tops, banked hits and 400-foot spines.

The Lions

descended upon him and eventually agreed that they were opposed to marijuana, but had no consistent policy with regard to the use of the substance in sports. Rebagliati kept his medal and found himself on the Tonight Show with host Jay Leno. There, he joked that his reaction to testing positive was "holy smokes". As for giving up his friends, Ross reasoned, "I may have to wear a gas mask, but I'll never give up my friends."

Golf in Vancouver

Each August, the PGA Greater Vancouver Open expects just about any PGA cardholder not at the World Series competition to show up and compete for a $1.5 million purse. For a

Downhill Ski Hills

Ski Report: (604) 299-9000, extension 3070.

Address/phone	No. of runs	Lift capacity/hour	Vertical drop	Selected services
Blackcomb Mountain (604) 932-3141	100 +	29,000	5,350 feet	Major side-by-side ski resorts, full ski & snowboard facilities including Fate-Half-pipe, Whistler Pipe, terrain parks, restaurants and lounges, shopping, kids camps, rentals, guides, races, beginners to advanced
Whistler Mountain, Whistler; (604) 932-3210 or 299-9000 and ext. 7547	100 +	30,000	5,020 feet	
Cypress Bowl, Hollyburn Mountain in West Vancouver, (604) 926-5612 or 299-9000, extension 2695	23	5,000	1,540 feet	Cafeteria, ski and snowboard schools, kids lessons, trails and warming hut, rentals, terrain park, shop
Grouse Mountain Resort, 6400 Nancy Green Way, North Vancouver; (604) 984-0661 or 299-9000, extension 6611	24	6,600	1,600 feet	Restaurants, ski, snowboard park, helicopter tours, night skiing, sleigh rides, women's lessons, disabled programs, kids lessons
Hemlock Valley, Agassiz in the Fraser Valley; (604) 797-4411	34	4,000	1,200 feet	Kids lessons, ski, snowboard pipes, shop, rentals, food store, races, lounge, cafeteria, RV hookups
Seymour Ski Country, 1700 Mount Seymour Road in North Vancouver; (604) 986-2261 or 299-9000, extension 7669	21	5,220	1,120 feet	Ski and snowboard, rentals, lessons, lounge, halfpipe, terrain park

Public Golf Courses In or Near the City of Vancouver

Last minute Golf Hotline: (604) 878-1833. For general information on golf equipment and supplies, call (604) 299-9000, extension 9761.

Golf course	Amenities reserve time	Advance
Ambleside Par 3 Golf Course, 1200 Marine Drive, West Vancouver, (604) 922-3818	18 holes, 1,204 yards, par 54, tight fairways set in a park, quick playing, equipment rentals	
Burnaby Mountain Golf Course, 7600 Halifax, Burnaby, (604) 421-8355	18 holes, par 71, 6,431 yards, undulating peat bog, desert, pro shop, driving range	2 days
Fraserview Golf Course, 7800 Vivian Drive, Vancouver, (604) 257-6921	18 holes, 6,700 yards, par 72, tree lined, revamped in 1998	5 days
Furry Creek Golf and Country Club, Lions Bay, North Shore, (604) 922-9461 ext. 235, or (604) 896-2216 ext. 235	18 holes, par 72, 6,001/5,861 yards, target golf, putting greens, lockers, practice facility, restaurant	10 days
Gleneagles Golf Course, 6190 Marine Drive, West Vancouver, (604) 921-7353	9 holes, 2,600 yards, par 71, café, pro shop, mountain and ocean views	First come, first served
Langara Golf Course, 290 West 49th Vancouver Parks and Recreation, 6706 Alberta St., Vancouver, (604) 280-1818	18 holes, 6,085 yards, par 71, tricky greens, pro shop, clubhouse, rating 68.8	5 days
McCleery Golf Course, Vancouver Parks and Recreation, 7188 MacDonald St., Vancouver, (604) 257-8191 or (604) 280-1818	18 holes, 6,265 yards, par 71, 30-stall driving range, pro shop, clubhouse, rating 69.6	5 days
Murdo Fraser Par 3 Golf Course, 2700 Pemberton, North Vancouver, (604) 980-8410	Par three, equipment rentals	First come, first served
Musqueam Golf Club and Training Centre, 3904 West 51st Ave, Vancouver, foot of Dunbar, (604) 266-2334	18 holes, par 60, 3,322 yards, scenic, 80 stall two-deck driving range	First come, first served
Northlands Golf Course, 3400 Anne MacDonald Way, North Vancouver (604) 280-1111	18 holes, 6,504 yards, par 71, new course in an old growth forest, level greens	3 days
Queen Elizabeth Pitch and Putt, 33rd Avenue off Cambie, Vancouver, (604) 874-8336	18 holes, par 54, 1,370 equipment rentals	First come, first served
Riverside Golf Centre Driving Range, 740 Marine Drive, North Vancouver, North Shore, (604) 980-4711	Driving range only, equipment sales	First come, first served
Riverside Golf Centre Driving Range, 820 SW Marine Drive, Vancouver, (604) 327-8077	Driving range only, equipment sales	First come, first served
Riverway Public Golf Course, 9001 Riverway Place, Burnaby, (604) 280-4653	18 holes, par 72, 7,010 yards, challenging dunes, driving range, pro shop, clubhouse, dining room and cafe, showers, lockers	2 days
Seymour Golf & Country Club 3723 Mt. Seymour Parkway, North Vancouver (604) 929-2611 or (604) 929-5491	18 holes, 6,291 yards, par 72	4 days
Stanley Park Pitch and Putt, near 2099 Beach Ave, Vancouver, (604) 681-8847	18 holes, 1,200 yards, par 54	First come, first served
University Golf Club, 5185 University Boulevard, Vancouver, (604) 224-1818	18 holes, 6,584 yards, par 72, mature course with trees, CPGA golf instruction, practice facility	1 week

week, enthusiastic, well-be-haved crowds watch the pros swing. First held in Vancouver in 1996, about 30 major sponsors and numerous smaller ones serve the 120,000+ spectators who attend. Major sponsors include Air Canada and TSN television network, which provides up to 13 hours of broadcast time. This PGA tourney helps to promote Canadian golf and golfers. For information on this year's mid-August PGA tournament, phone Northview Golf and Country Club, (604) 576-4653.

The Pacific Open, one of two majors on the Canadian Professional Golf Tour, is held in early June. For information on this year's particulars, contact the Mayfair Lakes Golf & Country Club, (604) 276-0505.

For golfers who just want to get to the links, a daily shuttle service offers daily golf packages door-to-door from several Vancouver hotels to top local courses. Join the morning shuttle (8:00 a.m. pick-up) or the afternoon shuttle (11:00 a.m. pick-up) to play the course of the day. The package includes green fees, cart, professional quality clubs and transportation from your hotel. Accessories such as rubber slip-ons with turf grips, rain jackets, umbrellas, hats and sunscreen are provided, so you are comfortable even if you came unprepared to play golf. Prices range from $80 to $150, depending on the course, season and day of the week. The Shuttle Hot Line at (604) 878-6800 is open 24 hours for information.

Hikers at Lighthouse Park on the North Shore

Easy Walks in Vancouver's Rainforests

Listed here are some of the easiest trails to explore on a sunny day.

For information on guided hikes and short day trips, call the Federation of Mountain Clubs of BC, (604) 878-7007.

Capilano River Regional Park in North Vancouver is a strip of land left in its original forested state beside a raging, whitewater river. The well-kept park trails meander through the misty rainforest. A bonus to any visit here is the salmon enhancement facility, a free display attraction just

below the Cleveland Dam. The whole trail runs for about 7 km (4.5 miles), though you may not wish to go the whole way. The largest tree, a Douglas fir, is about 2.4 m (8 feet) in diameter and is thought to be about 500 years old. Enter the park along Capilano Road where the signs guide you. The trail entrance is to the left of the salmon facility.

Capilano Suspension Bridge and park on the North Shore offers one of the easiest jaunts into the woods over a spectacular suspension bridge, formerly known as "the laughing bridge." After a look at the local history exhibits, there are concession stands and a souvenir store that stocks quality Canadiana. Admission is charged and there are several special events year-round. Enter from Capilano Road in North Vancouver, (604) 985-7474.

Lighthouse Park on the North Shore offers a marvelous diversity of habitats ranging from deep old growth rainforest to precipitous cliffs, rocky shore outcroppings and sheltered ocean coves. The granite outcroppings with

Skate Parks in and near Vancouver

Burnaby	**Burnaby** at Hastings and Willingdon, near the miniature railroad is outdoor concrete and as phalt, tranny and round lip, street obstacles, banks, escalator ledge.
Ladner	**Ladner** is located at 4600 Clarence Taylor Cres. net to the Recreation Centre. It is outdoor concrete, with a big wedge bank, bank with quarter pipe in middle, pyramids, ledges, stairs, handrail, escalator ledge.
Langley	**Langley** skate park is located at 203rd St. just off 64th Ave. It is an outdoor conrete with big wedge banks, a couple of pyramids and a fun box.
New Westminster	Located midway between 8th Ave. and 10th Ave. on 6th St., it is an outdoor concrete park with a maze of banks, bowls, ledges and ditches and a four-sided square-topped quarter pipe.
North Vancouver	**Griffin** is located at 351 W. Queens St., and is outdoor concrete, spacious ditch area with banks into a short snake run, finishing in a seven foot deep bowl, with lots of round lips.
	Parkgate is located next to parkgate Community centre, 3625 banff Court. Freestyle area with mini quarter, wedge bank, pyramid with flat bar, eight foot keyhole joined at one side with a spine to mini half with capsule end; joined at the other side with a mini half with capsule end, continuous metal coping throughout.
	Seylynn is an outdoor concrete park located at Mountain Highway and Hunter. It has a mini ditch into a snake run with four hips and a bowl at the bottom, good speed lines.
Richmond	Skate park is located on River Rd. near Lynas Lane and No. 2 Road bridge. It is concrete and as phalt, has three quarter pipes, two sets of stairs with rails, three other rails, a pyramid, sppine, funbox, three banks and a concrete half pipe.
Surrey	Located on King George Hwy. at 84th Ave. at Bear Creek. It is an outdoor concrete and asphalt park with horseshoe embankment, big pyramid, volcano, steps and handrail.
	South Surrey Bowl skate park is located next to the ice arena and baseball park at 146th Street and 20th Avenue. A $123,000 addition was just constructed.
Vancouver	**China Creek** at Broadway Ave. and Clark St. in East vancouver has an outdoor concrete, bathtub bow, mini keyhole bowl.
	Hastings is located at the Pacific National Exhibition north of Renfrew between PNE buildings and public park. It has two mini horseshoe bowls leading into snake run/half pipe, leading into ten foot deep bowl with two feet of vertical, continuous metal coping.
	Leeside is a covered park located at Hastings and Cassiar. It has masonite banks and ramps, a couple of pyramids, fun box, mini, new concrete.
West Vancouver	**Ambleside Park**, is outdoor concrete and asphalt, with big banks, planters, ledges of varying heights and a metal wheelchair ramp.
White Rock	Park is located at 146 St. and 20 Ave. This has a snake run leading to a deep bowl, hips, rails and banks.
Skate Shops	**Hot Shop** has a registry of all 20 skate parks in Greater Vancouver. 2868 West 4th St., (604) 739-7796. **Division Skate & Snow Shop**, 505 Dunsmuir, (604) 687-4935. **Hot Shop**, 2868 West 4th St., (604) 739-7796. **The Boardroom Snowboard Shop**, 1745 W 4th, (604) 734-7669. **The Board Kennel**, 1504 Foster, White Rock; (604) 535-7287. **Paul's Boutique**, 13630 108 Ave., Surrey (604) 951-7597

grooves that were left by the last glaciation period offer a great place for the kids to scramble. Blue grouse, woodpeckers and harlequin ducks are abundant. Adjacent to the park are Klootchman Park, a good vantage point from which to see surfbirds, and the lovely Caulfield Cove, a sandy strip where birds are also abundant. The Lighthouse, built in 1912, is closed to the public. Located near Beacon Lane just off Marine Drive in West Vancouver, a map near the entrance shows the trails.

Seymour Demonstration Forest in North Vancouver is 5,600 ha (13,900 acres) of living rainforest where folks of any age can learn about all things forest-related from wildlife to watershed management. Explore the easy trails deep in the woods on your own. In the summer, there are also guided walking treks and periodic bus tours available. Located along Fern St. near Capilano College in North Vancouver, phone ahead for information, (604) 987-1273 or for free Watershed Tours, contact (604) 432-6430.

Rockwood Adventures is a West Vancouver tour company offering guided eco-tours by land, sea and air with wine and food included at reasonable rates. Free pickup at most downtown hotels is a convenient service for those without a private vehicle. Phone for information; (604) 926-7705 or 1-888-236-6606. CNN, NBC and National Geographic Traveler have given favourable reviews.

Stanley Park Trails are fun to explore in the most renowned of Vancouver's parks. The ecosystem encompasses marine foreshore, coniferous forest, lakes, streams and formal gardens within its 400 ha (1,000 acres). Coyotes still roam the park as do overfed raccoons, squirrels and skunks. Seals and sea lions bask offshore. Guided nature walks are held periodically throughout the summer months. Enter from Georgia St. near Lost Lagoon Fountain; (604) 683-2000. See page 66.

Yew Lake Nature Trail on the North Shore is a summer-only self-guided level interpretive trail, about 1.5 km in length, highlighted by high-altitude forests, wildflower meadows and small lakes. The suggested walking time is 45 minutes. Located in Cypress Provincial Park, you can access it via a paved highway to the top of the mountain, then continue on foot. Cross Lions Gate Bridge to North Shore, take Highway 1 and exit on Cypress Park turnoff. Follow the road through the mixed Douglas fir forest to the ski area.

Spectacular by Nature

To explore the best places for birds, animals, insects, marine life and the most botanically interesting plants and wildflowers requires that you drive just outside Vancouver to its nearby environs. If you can sort out the phases of the moon, a worthwhile experience is the Full Moon Dyke Walk at Garry Point Park.

Burnaby Lake and Deer Lake in Vancouver's adjacent municipality of Burnaby are two waterways joined together. This area is home to 200 plant species; 200 bird species; 31 mammal species; 13 fish species; and 16 reptile and amphibian species. The best place to let kids feed inquisitive waterfowl is at Burnaby Lake. Enter at the foot of Piper Ave. off Government Road, Burnaby. The main lake trail joins this spot. For information, stop at the Nature House at 4519 Piper St., Burnaby. Summer kids' programs are available and for adults, low-cost, quick, how-to-canoe programs are held periodically; call (604) 420-3031.

Burns Bog, a 4,000 ha (9,800 acre) raised-dome peat bog, is a result of the last glaciation period. Described as the " lungs of the Lower Mainland," this ecological wetland gem is a crucial habitat for many kinds of creatures. Start at the Great Pacific Forum, 10388 Nordel Court, North Delta. Periodic guided tours and quick educational programs are available; phone ahead, Burns Bog Conservation Society, (604) 572-0373.

Camosun Bog, a small sphagnum bog, is possibly the oldest bog in the Lower Main-

Birdwatching is a feature of any forest hike

land. Plants such as Labrador tea, swamp laurel, insectivorous sundew and cloudberry thrive in the high water table. Located on Camosun St. just past 19th avenue, a trail and boardwalk make for quick and easy access. Information is available from Pacific Spirit Regional Park, (604) 224-5739.

Garry Point Park, at Steveston in Richmond, is an oceanside delta best viewed on nights when the full moon forms long, slippery, silver reflections in the water. First, determine the phase of the moon. If it is full or nearly so and the night is clear, plan on a fish and chips dinner at the picturesque oceanside wharf at one of the restaurants at Steveston Dockside, (604) 277-9511. Then, as the moon rises, walk westward from 7th Ave. and Chatham St., Richmond along the dyke and into the narrow park. The effect is unforgettable. Snow geese as well as raptors make this seaside marsh their home; (604) 271-8280 ofr Tourism Richmond.

Grant Narrows Regional Park on the city outskirts offers an opportunity in the winter months to see the magnificent trumpeter swans. All year round, waterfowl live in and around a huge freshwater lake. Pitt Lake is a body of water strangely affected by ocean tide backflows. Bird-viewing towers and signs showing the trails help visitors along. Canoe rentals are legendary.

BC Trees

Western red cedar and yellow cedar once provided aboriginal people with wood for houses, totem poles, dugout canoes and bent boxes, fibrous bark for woven baskets, hats and clothing, sheets of bark for roofing, inner bark for mats, fish traps and rope, and roots for rope and coiled baskets.

Natives used alder bark for dyes ranging from bright red-orange to dark brown.

Today, scientists are actively testing the use of Pacific yew as a potent anti-cancer drug.

Western hemlock pitch was once used for poultices and lineaments as well as mixed with deer tallow to prevent sunburn. Western hemlock is not poisonous and can be used to make delicious tea.

Douglas fir grows primarily on wet slopes after major fires and individual trees can live for over a thousand years. Many of the giant Douglas firs alive today represent the aftermath of fires that swept through this region several centuries ago.

The noble fir was used in World War II to build the frame of the R.A.F.'s Mosquito aircraft.

The Sitka spruce wood is light for its strength and was used to make frames for aircraft such as Howard Hugh's *Spruce Goose*.

The western white pine used to be a prevalent species in local forests. However, white pine blister rot was accidentally introduced from France in 1910 and by 1922, most of the great stands of white pines were dead.

Cedar trees cease to grow above the 300 m (1,000 foot) elevation line. It is believed their lead branches are easily broken by the weight of snow.

Yellow cedar, also called yellow cypress, can grow can attain an age of 1,000 to 1,500 years.

Unlike the birch trees growing in eastern North America, paper birch or white birch bark from trees in British Columbia is too weak to make canoes. Aboriginals used its resin as chewing gum.

The red, bark-shedding arbutus tree is known as the madrone in the United States.

101

Location: Pitt Lake off DeKoster Road, Renie Road or Koerner Road; Dewdney-Alouette Parks, (604)460-8300.

Jericho Beach Park is a good city location for birding. Within its 54 ha (130 acres), about 180 species of birds make their home within its mix of woodland, marsh, pond, sandy and saltwater settings. Gulls, herons and eagles (in winter) feed along the exposed sand flats. Located on the north side of West 4th Ave, there are entrances at Wallace or Discovery streets, Vancouver. Information is available from the Vancouver information centre, (604) 683-2000.

Musqueum Park is quite small but offers access to Blenheim Flats and Southlands, semi-rural areas cutting through two golf courses. Walking trails meander through a western red cedar and hemlock forest. Musqueum Park is on 46th and Highbury near Crown St. Information is available from the Vancouver information centre, (604) 683-2000.

OWL, The Orphaned Wildlife Rehabilitation Centre in Delta, is open to the public on Saturdays and Sundays from 10 a.m. to 3 p.m. The recipient of a number of environmental awards, OWL treats more than 200 injured birds of prey each year with a 70 per cent success rate for release. Bev Day, director, had over 25 eagles and hawks brought into her shelter over a recent six month period. "The pesticides are travelling up the food chain from ducks, seagulls and pigeons to the eagles." While she believes

Jericho Beach Park

there is a need for change, Bev Day also states, "We can't blame farmers for providing us with the fruit and vegetables that we're buying without complaints." Special open house days occur in summer; (604) 946-3171; telephone for the address.

Richmond Nature Park touts its boggy environment and offers some of the best nature programs and walks for children and/or adults. The adjoining Nature House has interesting amateur displays and in autumn, blueberries are abundant. Though much-touted, the endless shubbery along the

bark mulch trails can become repetitive. Location: 11851 Westminster Highway, Richmond. Call for information about current Richmond Nature Park guided programs, held throughout the Lower Mainland, (604) 273-7015.

Reifel Migratory Bird Sanctuary is located some distance from downtown, but is worth a visit. Its teeming waterfowl, including snow geese and trumpeter swans, are spectacular in the winter. Open from 9 a.m. to 4 p.m. daily, the protected sanctuary is located 8 km (6 miles) west of Ladner on Westham Island, Delta. This facility attracts

Great blue heron

Fishing Tips

Fisheries and Oceans Canada has Salmon updates and regulations at (604) 299-9000 ext. 3467. Policy and Communications Branch is (604) 666-0384.

For Vancouver/Howe Sound saltwater fish tips, contact **Sewell's Marina**, 6695 Nelson in Horseshoe Bay, (604) 921-3474 or 299-9000 ext. 7027.

Hanson's Fishing Outfitters provides rods, reels, tackle and supplies for salt and freshwater fishing, and they arrange half- or full-day charters. Drop into 580 Hornby St., Vancouver, or phone (604) 684-8988.

West Coast Fishing Tackle, 2147 East Hastings near Victoria, (604) 254-0004.

birders from around the world. Headquarters are found at 5191 Robertson Road, Ladner; (604) 946-6980.

The University of British Columbia Botanical Garden, occupying 24 ha (60 acres), is one of the oldest botanical research facilities in Canada. Started in 1911, its present collection of Asian plants, extensive alpine specimens, and Physick Garden of medicinal plants make it a fascinating visit. The native plant garden showcases indigenous BC specimens. As a bonus, this garden's situation on a ocean bluff makes it a good place to spot bald eagles, horned owls, blackbirds, ravens, and Rufous hummingbirds. Located at 6804 SW Marine Drive on the U.B.C. campus, volunteers conduct guided tours of the gardens from

time to time; phone for times, (604) 822-9666.

VanDusen Botanical Garden presents a collection of well-managed plants, illustrating both Asian opulence and native plant diversity. There are comprehensive collections of southern hemisphere plants, rhododendrons, heather and holly bushes. In addition, every garden club, association and society holds a show or two here each year; phone ahead to find out what is happening. Allow three hours to view this garden. Located at 37th Ave. and Oak St., volunteers occasionally conduct guided tours of the gardens. Phone for times, (604) 878-9274. Open 10 a.m. to 6 p.m. daily.

Vancouver Restaurants

Vancouver's diverse restaurants invite diners to enjoy their tempting specialties

T he delights of West Coast cuisine are a bit difficult to quantify, but they seem to combine a decor that crackles with excitement and a choice of foods so fresh they almost wiggle. The following describes some of the city's "hot spots"; reservations are always recommended.

Barbecued salmon combined with a city overlook:

Salmon House on the Hill, 2229 Folkestone Way, West Vancouver on the North Shore, (604) 926-3212, keeps it

It Pays to Know

All meals are subject to 7 per cent G.S.T. and 10 per cent Liquor Tax.

Suggested average tipping is 15 per cent before taxes.

Last call is at 1 a.m. and licensed establishments must be vacated by 2 a.m.

simple with a winning combination of alder-smoked salmon and various desserts set against twinkling city lights. This is a favorite place for Vancouver residents to take their out-of-town guests.

Best First Nations food, adapted to contemporary tastes:

Liliget Feast House and Catering, 1724 Davie St., near Denman, (604) 681-7044, was awarded four stars by the *New York Times* newspaper. It is Vancouver's only First Nations restaurant, and specializes in Potlatch platters

and native cuisine.

Best place to celebrate West Coast cuisine on a very special evening:

Bishop's, 2183 West 4th St., (604) 738-2025, will offer you fine wine and contemporary West Coast cooking at its best.

Best food and all-round West Coast people-watching experience:

O'Doul's Restaurant & Bar, 1300 Robson St., (604) 661-1400, is the place to spend an evening if you're in the mood for an exciting menu, West Coast decor, jazz on the weekends and the overall feeling

left: Canada Place from Stanley Park

you have really arrived in Vancouver.

Best authentic, inventive West Coast cuisine:
RainCity Grill, 1193 Denman St., (604) 685-7337, makes fusions of California and Pacific Northwest cuisine and a fine choice of award-winning Pacific northwest wines. An extended version of this famous and popular restaurant is now located in Raintree at the Landing, 375 Water St. in Gastown, (604) 688-5570.

Most inventive seafood menu:
The Fish House, 8901 Stanley Park Drive, (604) 681-7275, invites you to try wood-oven-roasted calamari or a seafood hot pot among its other innovative specialties.

Best seafood with a harbour view:
The Cannery, 2205 Commissioner St. near Victoria Drive, (604) 254-9606, offers glimpses of the fleet and tastes of the day's catch. Try the grilled halibut cheeks or steamed smoked Alaskan black cod with butter.

Asian Restaurants
In Vancouver, many hundreds of establishments offer fresh food authentically prepared in distinctive styles of the orient that were many thousands of years in the making. There are two ways to discover your own Asian food experience: one is to walk through Chinatown along Pender and Keefer streets. The second is to seek out a specific type of cuisine from the choices below.

Best Cantonese fare by Hong Kong chefs:
Imperial Chinese Seafood

Restaurant, The Marine Building, 355 Burrard St. at Hastings, (604) 688-8191, has a wondrous view of Coal Harbour. Eating here is like having high tea in a grand ballroom of the past. Dim sum service is excellent. Dinner can be just as engaging—lobster in black bean sauce with noodles, or sautéed spinach with minced pork.

Best dim sum:
Grand King Seafood, 705 West Broadway at Heather, (604) 876-7855, offers extensive dim sum choices in a big, boxy restaurant. The chefs impress their clientele with traditional southern favorites and country-style cooking including whole Dungeness crab; lettuce wrap steamed and stuffed with shrimp mousse, crisp-roasted chicken Canton, or a generous pot of the best chicken congée. Reservations are compulsory.

Park Lock Seafood Restaurant, 544 Main St. in Chinatown, (604) 688-1581. This restaurant serves dim sum and long-standing favorites such as black pepper flank steak, scallops and prawns with black bean sauce and

hard-to-find spareribs in yellow-plum sauce.

Best Korean cuisine:
Seoul House Royal, 1215 West Broadway, (604) 739-9001, is the largest and busiest Korean restaurant in Canada. It is remarkable for its barbecue dishes and karaoke sing-alongs.

Best shoestring-budget Chinese:
Hon's Wun-Tun House, 268 Keefer St., (604) 688-0871, offers little in the way of atmosphere but plenty of slurpy noodles and low-budget potstickers.

Best Southeast Asian cuisine:
Vij's, 1480 W. 11th (604) 736-6664, is popular. No reservations.

Phnom Penh, two locations, 1) 955 West Broadway, (604) 734-8898, (604) 734-8988; 2) 244 E. Georgia, (604) 682-5777. This establishment was chosen by visiting celebrity Julia Child to taste its down-to-earth country cooking specialties from Vietnam and Cambodia. Consistently award-winning Cambodian fare includes exemplary hot

Java Jabber

Café au lait
1.5 ounces espresso and three ounces steamed milk

Café latté
1.5 ounces espresso in a six-ounce cup filled with steamed milk and topped with foam

Café mocha
Espresso, chocolate syrup, steamed milk, whipped cream, cocoa powder

Cappuccino
1.5 ounces espresso in a six-ounce cup half filled with steamed milk, topped with a peak of foamed milk

Double tall skinny
Double espresso and steamed nonfat milk

Espresso
1.5 ounces served in a three-ounce demitasse

Frappuccino or iced cappuccino
Ice cold café au lait in a 12-ounce glass

and sour soups; unbeatable garlic-pepper squid, prawns, crab, or cooked-to-perfection lemongrass chicken.

Best Malaysian cuisine:

Tropika, 3105 West Broadway, (604) 737-6002, specializes in vibrant satay dishes from this exotic land such as simple Sotong Kang Kong.

The Banana Leaf, 1020 West Broadway, (604) 731-6333, a neighbourhood favorite, is home to excellent Malaysian cuisine such as the fluffy roti canai appetizers with curry garnish.

Best encyclopedic "Chinese" cuisine:

Kirin, 102, 1166 Alberni St., (604) 682-8833, offers good fare from all regions of China. Dim sum daily. Look for rich, sweet, red-cooked dishes from the north and the best Peking duck pastry on this side of the Pacific. Fresh seasonal seafood choices such as drunken live spot prawns and whole Alaskan king crab are presented with dramatic tableside special effects.

Pink Pearl, 1132 East Hastings St., (604) 253-4316, provides a classic atmosphere in which to enjoy a variety of hot and sour soups, Peking duck or numer-

ous other specialties. With its 650 seats, it continues to be a Vancouver favourite. Dim sum is a point-and-buy funfest of cultural immersion.

Best Thai dishes:

Thai House, 1116 Robson St., (604) 683-3383, was a recent and deserving winner of *Vancouver* magazine's Best Asian Restaurant award. Beneath abundant skylights, Thai cuisine delights diners with curry, ginger and spoonfuls of garlic. Try chicken in coconut milk and yellow curry, or deep-fried cod with hot sauce.

Sala Thai Restaurant, 3364 Cambie St., (604) 875-6999. This establishment also deliv-

The Coffee Thing

Right from the get-go and being only a stone's throw from Seattle (America's coffee capital), Vancouver embraced all the delicate nuances of the coffee "thing." Learn a little java jabber and you will enhance your enjoyment of this ritual immeasurably. This industry's marketing strategies offer trendy insights into modern consumers. For example, here are a few trade secrets: the coffee bar can be any colour but green (negative food associations); lighting must be cosy but bright enough for stockbrokers or poets to read by; women make 70 per cent of gourmet-coffee purchases; written announcements purporting "freshly brewed" coffee inadvertently destroy the impression that fresh coffee is always available; handing a cup to a customer increases the chance of spilling so cups are placed onto a counter; no matter how much they earn, the

best-educated customers drink the most specialty coffee. Join the crowd.

Most consistent standard-setting coffee house:

Starbucks continues to set the pace for all its competitors and is a good place to experience a reliable bit of the specialty-coffee scene. Found throughout Greater Vancouver in more than 85 locations, the most notable anchor-establishments occupy two corners of the same busy Robson Street intersection, 1099 Robson St., (604) 685-1099.

Best selection of goodies with excellent coffee:

Bread Garden Bakery & Cafés are found in a dozen locations including the one at 1040 Denman St., (604) 685-2996.

Best-established coffee seller:

Murchies Tea & Coffee Ltd. hearkens back to 19th century days

when billowing clipper ships still called into the port of Vancouver straight from the exotic Orient. This importer knows coffee and tea well and the aromas floating about their establishments have inspired generations of java lovers. Try one of the 10 Murchies outlets at 970 Robson St., (604) 669-2649.

Best place to shoot pool and drink specialty coffee:

Benny's Bagels provides a post-modern experience at 1780 Davie St., (604) 685-7600, at 2505 West Broadway, (604) 731-9730 or at 3365 Cambie St., (604) 872-1111.

Best place to satisfy a chocolate craving:

Sutton Place Hotel provides a chocolate feast on Thursday, Friday and Saturday nights at 6:00 p.m. and 8:30 p.m. 845 Burrard St., (604) 682-5511.

ers regional dishes like prawn soup or green curried chicken prepared to individual tastes from mild to spicy hot.

Best eastern Chinese regional classics:
Shanghai Garden Restaurant, 3932 Fraser St., (604) 873-6123, is famous for its "drunken" (wine-drenched) chicken; crispy deep-fried duck; silky pan-fried tofu on spinach; exemplary potstickers; and chili-fried Dungeness crab.

Best X.O. sauce:
Fortune Restaurant 608-650 W. 41st Ave., (604) 266-7728, is an upscale Oakridge restaurant famous for a superior chili dip condiment, X.O. sauce, spiked with conpoy, dried mushrooms and shrimps, as well as an innovative menu including singing chicken in Mandarin wine sauce, and a good dim sum service.

Best do-it-yourself Asian-style cooking:
Landmark Hotpot House, 4023 Cambie St., (604) 872-2868, offers picture-perfect presentation and uncompromised freshness. A gas stove set into your table provides the basis for do-it-yourself fondue-style cooking. Start with the live prawns, then finish with the noodles and dumplings and a bowl of rich broth.

Enough good Asian food to feed four to six for $50:
Wonton King, 620 S.E. Marine Dr., (604) 321-4433, is famous for its crispy spareribs in salt and chilies, or the velvety hand-shredded chicken.

Best Buddhist vegetarian:
Buddhist Vegetarian Restaurant, 137 Pender St. (604) 683-8816, features mock meats fashioned from clever manip-

ulations of wheat gluten and soybean sheets for a complex menu of 130-plus vegetarian and vegan dishes. Try it first in small doses; it is not for everyone.

Best Japanese cuisine:
Tojo, 202-777 W, Broadway (604) 872-8050, is consistently rated the top Japanese—especially the sushi.

Kamei Royal, 2nd floor, 1030 West Georgia St., enter off Burrard (604) 687-8588, offers tempting sashimi, teriyaki and more from the crowded bar or in the comfort of private tatami mat rooms.

Shijo Japanese Restaurant, 1926 West 4th Avenue, (604) 732-4676.

Yoshi, 1925 W. 4th Ave. (604) 738-8226, is an emerging favourite.

Chiyoda Japanese Restaurant, 200-1050 Alberni St., (604) 688-5050; or Kakiemon

Restaurant, 200 Burrard St., (604) 688-6866.

Best show of noodle making:
Shanghai Chinese Bistro, 1124 Alberni St., (604) 683-8222, is a bright, trend-setting restaurant featuring spicy chili prawns, white-cooked pork with garlic, excellent dumplings and a highly entertaining nightly show of the art of noodle-making.

Best Szechuan cuisine on a budget:
Szechuan Chongqing, 2808 Commercial Drive, (604) 254-7434, offers the best but infamously incendiary garlic and chili pepper dishes.

Best Chiuchow-style noodles:
Mui Garden Restaurant, 4265 Main St., (604) 872-8232, is a simple neighbourhood noodle shop offering excellent noodles as well as cuttlefish and beef meatballs, Singapore satays, curries or Hi Nan chicken plus hot pot specials of lamb, singing chicken or Hong Kong

West Coast Cuisine Basics

To enjoy the best dining during your West Coast visit, plan your culinary adventures with these ideas in mind.

Asian flavours
From Korean hot pots to East Indian curries, from Chinese southern to northern flavours, specialized authentic Asian cuisine is found throughout Vancouver.

British Colombia wines
Award winning, fine tasting and mature, BC wines are second to none.

Fresh flavours and herbs; exotic vegetables
West Coast cooking is renowned for its "fresh from the garden" appeal.

Local micro-brewed beers
Beers are specially brewed to appeal to those who like clear, cold, fizzy lagers.

Traditional Native foods
Adapted to contemporary tastes From oolichans to soapberry ice-cream and wild game, there are new taste sensations to try.

Salmon and seafood, West Coast style
A quick dip of the net and it is fresh on your plate, enrobed in a low calorie, high impact sauce.

satay beef studded with pineapple.

Best value-for-quality sushi:
Shijo, 202,1926 West Fourth Ave., (604) 732-4676, is the place for grilled mushrooms in foil, cones stuffed with prawn tempura, or the robata grill, as well the hundreds of sushi choices.

Microbreweries

No Canadian experience is complete without a bit of appreciation for Canadian beers. Attracting a great deal of favorable attention and adding to the legend are several local microbreweries. They brew up a number of special-interest beers and ales. Giant conglomerates, ever alert to public appetites, also market with their own special brands. It seems that "Beauty lies in the hands of the beerholder."

Lines have increasingly blurred between restaurants, breweries and pubs as all three types of establishments cater to the same micro-brew-appreciating clients. Syndicated columnist Dave Barry put it best: "Without question, the greatest invention in the history of mankind is beer. Oh, I grant you that the wheel was also a fine invention, but the wheel does not go nearly as well with pizza."

Microbrews and the Establishments that Promote Them

Beer as suave as a row of head waiters:
Granville Island Brewery, 1441 Cartwright St., under the Granville Street Bridge on Granville Island, (604) 687-2739, is owned by Casacadia Brands Inc. and brews beer according to the German Purity Law of 1516. With only four ingredients, choice two-row Canadian barley malt, fine German hops and special yeast, their Island Light brand is one of their claims to fame. Several daily tasting tours are held; phone for times. They also serve delicious food accompaniments.

Beers with a Norse bite like a frog wired up to a main switch:
Sailor Hägar's Brew Pub, 86 Semisch, North Vancouver, (604) 984-3087, serves hearty food along with its nine uncompromising brews. The experience is enhanced by a bonus view of the city skyline

across the harbour. Try the sampler ales, pilsners or wheat beer. Alternatively, the 12 per cent alcohol brew may hit the spot. Call ahead if you would like a tour of the adjacent brewery.

Brews as smooth as angels' wings:
Steamworks Brewing Co., 375 Water St. in Gastown, (604) 689-2739, is many visitors' favorite place to order a "designer" pizza and wash it down with Harvest Gold Ale or Nut Brown Nirvana. A fabulous pub-like atmosphere downstairs, or the view-laden, lounge-like upstairs complements a menu offering both continental fare and that of the Pacific Northwest.

Stylish brews for people watching:
Yaletown Brewing Co., 1111 Mainland, Vancouver, (604) 688-0039 or (604) 681-2739, offers brews made with the adventurous application of hops. Its Mainland Lager is cool and wonderful. Its Dunkel, a dark ale, is considered most worthy by beer aficionados. Offering charming, warehouse-style rooms, the eclectic, California-leanin' menu features six superior home brews. If your blackened chicken with Anaheim

Recognizing Micro-beer Brands

Capilano Brewing Co. is a subsidiary of the giant Molson's and is noted for its Ricard's Red.

Columbia Brewing Company is a subsidiary of the giant Labatt's and is noted for its Kootenay Black Lager and Kootenay Mountain Ale.

Okanagan Springs is owned by Sleeman Breweries from Guelph, Ontario and is famous for its Okanagan Springs Premium Lager and Old English Porter Ale.

Shaftebury Brewing Co., now part of Okanagan Springs, in addition to its Shaftebury Ales is becoming famous for its "ugly" beer, Honey Pale Ale, as pure as the driven slush, and its Hemp Ale.

R & B Brewing Co. features Red Devil Ale, Raven Ale, Sun God Wheat Ale and the seasonal Old Nick.

Storm Brewing Ltd. is a small brewery featuring unfiltered ales brewed in small batches. Brands are: Hurricane I.P.A., Black Plague Stout, Twister Wheat Ale, Highland Scottish Ale and Fruit Lambics.

peppers and sour cream or cilantro pizza is a little saltier than usual, a pint of Franks' Nut Brown Ale or Red Brick Bitter will cure the problem. Brewery tours are available.

Good selection of local beers and ales on Granville Island:
Bridges, 1696 Duranleau, (604) 687-4400, is the pub/restaurant with the yellow roof.

Good selection of local brews on the North Shore:
Pemberton Station, 135 Pemberton St. near the tracks, North Vancouver; (604) 984-3558, is a friendly pub in the old train station.

Seaside pub to watch ferry loading:
The Trollers, 6422 Bay, Horseshoe Bay, West Vancouver; (604) 921-7616, is a near the BC Ferry terminal and distributes products for Horseshoe Bay Brewing Co., as does nearby Ya Ya's restaurant.

Moderate food prices and fine beers:
The Fringe Café, 3124 West Broadway, (604) 738-6977, charges about the same amount for its entrées as trendy pubs ask for potato skins. Prices are similarly moderate for its 35 import beers, from Kenya's Tusker to India's Kingfisher, as well as five microbrewery beers on draught. Most notable is the very palatable house ale, Ugly Boy.

West Coast atmosphere and local brews:
Stamps Landing, 610 Stamps Landing at False Creek, (604) 879-0821, is a pub with 20 or more brews on tap.

Yaletown Brewing Co.

Creek Restaurant/Dockside Brewery, 1253 Johnston St. on Granville Island (604) 685-7070, has Dark Lager, Light lager, Dockside Pilsner nad Dockside Pale Ale.

Dix Barbecue and Brewery, 871 Beatty St. (604) 682-2739. Four house brews, mainly lagers.

Big River Brew Pub and Restaurant, 14200 Blvd., Richmond (604) 271-2739, has a décor based on the history of the Fraser River.

Best Bets for Vancouver Dining
If you are feeling hungry and confused, these listings should help you sort out those deep-seated longings. First, check out the West Coast cuisine listings on page 45. If you still feel peckish, try one of these. Reservations are always recommended, if appropriate, and the food at all these listings is reliably delicious.

Best "Vancouver" experience:
Aqua Riva, 200 Granville St., (604) 683-5599, combines vistas of cruise ships, wood-fired grilled foods, pizza or pastas, micro-brews, martinis or

champagne with the unmistakable feeling that it could not come together like this anywhere else in the world.

Best Asian and West Coast fusion cuisine:
C Restaurant, 1600 Howe St., (604) 681-1164, offers Saskatoon-berry- tea-cured salmon gravlax as a starter and continues to impress the palate as more courses are served.

Best breakfasts the old-fashioned way:
Bert's Restaurant, 2904 Main St., (604) 876-1236
Café Barney, 2975 Granville St., (604) 731-6446
Sophie's Cosmic Cafe, 2095 West Fourth Ave, (604) 732-6810.
Templeton, 1087 Granville St., (604) 685-4612, all have periodic lineups that attest to their desirability.

Best budget dining room:
JJ's Dining Room, Vancouver Community College, 250 West Pender St., (604) 443-8479, lets you be the guinea pig for cooking students. The best deal in town on Friday night.

Best celebrity hangout:
Cin Cin Ristorante, 1154 Robson St., (604) 688-7338, never

promises glimpses of the stars, but is high on every hotel concierge's secret recommendation list.

Best cheap thrill:
Gyoza King, 1508 Robson St., (604) 669-8278, is the master of plump dumplings and the flavours of Japan. It is open late.

Best Chinese food on a budget:
Shanghai Bistro, 1128 Alberni St., (604) 683-8222, is a noodle-maker with soul-satisfying Shanghai, Cantonese or Mandarin offerings.

Best East Indian spicy:
Dawat, 5076 Victoria Drive, (604) 322-3550, gets high marks for curried mussels in garlic sauce and dosas, Indian pancakes.

Best tapas:
Bin 942 Tapas Parlour, 1521 W. Broadway (604) 734-9421, features award winning scallops poached in icewine.

La Bodega, 1277 Howe St. (604) 684-8815, features a traditional tapas menu.

Most wicked margaritas, Olé!:
Las Margaritas, 1999 West 4th Ave., (604) 734-7117, brings all

the expected TexMex dishes in winningly renovated Kitsilano premises. There's a Mexican brunch on weekends.

Best fine Italian:
Gianni Norcineria, 2881 Granville St., (604) 738-7922, offers the high style game and truffles dishes that give sun-drenched Italy its warm ambiance.

Il Giardino di Umberto, 1382 Hornby St., (604) 669-2422, is another place to dine alfresco à la Tuscany, with entrées to match the atmosphere.

Best sangria by the pitcher and gringo-style Mexicali food:
Topanga Café, 2904 W. 4th Ave., (604) 733-3713, is a Kitsilano favorite. It is known for its garlicky homemade guacamole, salsa and chips and shredded-chicken enchiladas.

Best fish and chips:
Olympia Seafood Market and Grill, 820 Thurlow St., (604) 685-0716, offers you a choice of fishes and fresh cut fries.

Best French cuisine:
Le Crocodile, 100, 909 Burrard St., (604) 669-4298, also vies for top awards.

Best Greek food:
Kalamata Taverna, 478 West Broadway at Cambie, (604) 872-7050, is said to be touched by magic. It serves unbeatable souvlaki and unrivaled southern Greek home cooking.

Best healthy cuisine:
Picasso Café, 1626 West Broadway, (604) 732-3290, has a menu that lives according to HeartSmart guidelines and is great for dieting visitors too.

Best hole-in-the-wall:
Tokyo Joe's, 2825 West Broad-

Retrospective: Vancouver Restraint Trends

The "sin" trend, particularly as it related to male tastes, was on the rise. This included martinis and scotches, rotisseried steaks, cheese sauces and cigar lounges. Special rooms were even set aside to satisfy this pleasurable craving.

Revival of healthy foods continued unabated as visiting U.S. President Clinton discovered when he ordered not just a

vegetarian phyllo, but the "low fat, hold the goat cheese" variety. Demand for inspired vegetarian choices continued to grow.

The neighbourhood bistro in the suburbs offered a comfortable yet sophisticated friendliness. Lines blurred between restaurants, breweries and pubs as all three types of establishments catered to the same types of clients.

way, (604) 739-4791, and 955 Helmcken St. (604) 689-0073 is popular thanks to its tasty Japanese dishes and low prices.

Best "I can't make up my mind" place:
Roti Bistro, 1958 West Fourth Ave., (604) 730-9906, fuses Trinidad, East African, Portuguese and Chinese cuisines and offers cheap prices to boot.

Best "I feel like a great pizza" place:
Flying Wedge, 1205 Davie St., (604) 681-1288, has specialties like "Broken Heart" topped with artichokes and onions. also located at 200 Burrard St. (604) 681-1122, 1055 Georgia St. (604) 681-1233, 1166 Alberni St. (604) 681-1288, 345 Robson

St. (604) 689-7078, 1937 Cornwall Ave. (604) 732-8840 and 3499 Cambie St. (604) 874-8284.

Best "I feel like a steak tonight" place:
Mark's Steak and Taphouse, 2486 Bayswater St., (604) 734-1325, attracts the T-shirt crowd to its seven kinds of steak, including T- bone. It also serves pizza and pasta.

Best kid-friendly but still special:
Old Spaghetti Factory, 53 Water St., (604) 684-1288, serves home-style pasta in a warehouse atmosphere that has gone over very well for more than a generation.

Romano's Macaroni Grill at the Mansion, 1800 1st Ave., (604) 714-6500, will surprise the kids and please parents with understandable fare like chicken parmesan or pizza all set in a grand turn-of-the-century manor. Wine is charged according to how much you consume—they mark the side of the bottle!

Best outdoor dining on a warm summer night:
Monk McQueens, 601 Stamps Landing on False Creek, (604) 877-1351, has a lively, crowded terrace and great mountain and city views.

Best people watching:
Cactus Club Café, 1136 Robson St., (604) 687-3278, has tables

Vancouver's Best View Restaurants

If the view is what you're after, and you want to enjoy the elegant feeling of Vancouver's harbour and mountain setting, these fine restaurants are the best places. Also included are two companies that offer dinner cruises and wonderful views of the harbour.

Aqua Riva, 200 Granville Street, (604) 683-5599, house-smoked duck, shiitake mushrooms, French/continental seafood. Spectacular waterfront and lights, get a window seat.

Beach House, Dundarave Pier, 150-25th St., West Vancouver, (604) 922-1414, seafood Waterfront setting, distant lights of downtown and bridge, get a window seat.

Boomtown Tours Ltd., 750 Pacific Blvd. South, (604) 682-2070, harbour cruises and dinner Boat: waterside harbour views.

Fish House in Stanley Park, 8901 Stanley Park Drive, (604)

681-7275, grilled BC salmon with maple glaze, wood-oven roasted dishes, calamari. Views of the harbour and ships, lights; get a window seat.

The Riley Waterfront Cafe, 1661 Granville St., (604) 684-3666, plain continental fare Under the Granville Bridge, views of the water.

Harbour Cruises Ltd., No. 1 - North Foot of Denman St., (604) 687-9558, harbour cruises and dinner, boat and train trips There are great waterside harbour views.

Horizons, 100 Centennial Way, Burnaby, (604) 299-1155, West Coast seafood, New Mexican. Sweeping views from mountains to downtown, get a window seat.

Monk McQueen's Fresh Seafood and Oyster Bar, 601 Stamps Landing, (604) 877-1351, casual elegance, rack of lamb. Marine and water views in

False Creek, get a window seat.

Salmon House on the Hill, 2229 Folkstone Way, West Vancouver, (604) 926-3212, alder-grilled salmon.

Panorama of city lights and ships in the harbour, most seats are good.

Seasons in the Park, Queen Elizabeth Park, (604) 874-8008, West Coast cuisine. Cedar trees, lush garden, Vancouver's skyline, get a window seat.

The Cannery, 2205 Commissioner St., (604) 254-9606, warehouse decor, alder-grilled fish. Waterfront location, bottom of Victoria St., get a window seat.

The Five Sails, 999 Canada Place, (604) 891-2892, crab meat and caviar, Pacific Rim flavours. Elegant views of Stanley Park, city and mountains, get a window seat.

Borgo Antico, 321 Water St. in Gastown, (604) 683-8376, fine Italian. Harbour traffic, sit upstairs.

Canada Place Sails

outside to enjoy the steady stream of passers-by.

Best romantic brunch or dinner:

The Teahouse, Ferguson Point in Stanley Park, (604) 669-3281, is a dimly lit hunter's cottage in the cedar forest. It is especially rewarding after a long walk along the Seawall. Exceptional for either brunches or dinners.

Best romantic dinner on a train:

Pacific Starlight Dinner Train, BC Rail Station, 1311 West First Ave., North Vancouver, (604) 984-5246 or (604) 299-9000 ext. 3733, is a truly movable feast with wine, dinner and music on the way to Porteau Cove. Reservations are compulsory.

Best sophisticated dinner:

Cafe Il Nido, 780 Thurlow St., (604) 685-6436, offers a warm ambiance and Italian food in the formal classic setting of the Manhattan Building's courtyard.

Best scrumptious sandwiches:

Presto Panini, 859 Hornby St., (604) 684-4445, makes its offerings on plain or focaccia breads and serves them warm or chilled on fiestaware plates.

Tony's Neighbourhood Deli-Cafe, 1046 Commercial Drive, (604) 253-7422, takes hot, crusty bread and grills it with oozing mozzarella, caprese and sun-dried tomatoes among other wonderful creations.

Best tea and sandwiches:

The Secret Garden Tea Co., 5559 West Boulevard, (604) 261-3070, serves tiny tea sandwiches or big, bursting monsters with soup on the side.

Best teenage lure:

Hard Rock Café, 686 Hastings St., (604) 687-ROCK, is an internationally famous theme restaurant with a wacky, expensive menu. Reservations are compulsory.

Best twenty-something budget place:

Ouisi Bistro, 3014 Granville St., (604) 732-7550, has a jazz theme and good vibes for hangin' out.

Best view, 360 degrees:

Cloud Nine, 1400 Robson St. atop the Landmark Hotel, (604)687-0511, offers a sensational panorama.

Best vegetarian and funky food:

Planet Veg, 1941 Cornwall St., (604) 734-1001, tends toward Thai flavours like rice pots and is inexpensive.

Best vegetarian self-serve:

Woodlands, 2582 West Broadway, (604) 733-5411, is a perennial favorite with lots of inventive choices.

Important Visitor Information

Please buckle up: Drivers and all passengers in motor vehicles must, by law, use installed seat belts.

Vehicle entry: Though generally routine, visitors with rented vehicles should carry a copy of the rental contract endorsed for entry to Canada.

Vehicle insurance: U.S. motorists should check with their U.S. insurance company to be certain they meet minimum BC provincial coverage requirements.

Lock your car every time you leave it. Discreetly place all valuables and loose items in the trunk; deactivate the latch. Even the simplest objects, an old jacket (money in the pockets?) tapes or crumpled papers left exposed inside the car can invite thieves. Unfortunately, petty car break-ins and thefts in tourist areas are on the rise.

Money exchange: Visitors are encouraged to exchange their funds for Canadian dollars at a bank, credit union, or foreign currency exchange outlet. Credit card companies charge a premium exchange rate the day the transaction goes through their computers—often some days after the purchase is made. Many Canadian banks are open from 9 a.m. to 4 or 5 p.m.; limited hours on Saturdays; closed Sundays. Cash machines are common and will interact with many international services. Non-Canadian Banks back home will generally not accept Canadian coins.

Up-to-the-minute currency exchange rates: Phone (604) 299-9000, extension 3004.

Canadian coins include pennies, nickels, dimes, quarters, $1 "loonies" and $2 "toonies." Paper bills are not issued for $1 or $2 amounts.

Using U.S. dollars: Most Vancouver shops and restaurants accept U.S. dollars and grant a fair exchange rate only slightly less favourable than banks. However, this is never guaranteed.

Bank holidays: In the summer season the banks close as follows:

Victoria Day: late May—the Monday preceding May 24; Canada Day: July 1st; BC Civic Holiday: the first Monday in August; Labour Day: the first Monday in September. Bank cash machines remain open.

Distance is measured in kilometres. A kilometre is 5/8 of a mile; 100 kilometres are only 60 miles.

Gasoline is measured in litres (l). An American gallon is 4 l. To compare gas prices, multiply the Canadian price-per-litre by four. For British residents, an Imperial gallon is 5 l.

Temperature is measured in degrees Celsius (°C). Room temperature of 70 °F is 20 °C. What sounds like a cool day, say 30 °C, is actually scorching hot—in the 100 °F range. Outdoor temperatures of 15 °C to 25 °C are considered comfortably warm.

Weather update: For Vancouver, phone 299-9000, extension 3501.

Sales taxes: Both provincial sales tax of 7 per cent and a G.S.T. or federal sales tax of 7 per cent are charged on goods for a compound total of 15 per cent. The G.S.T. or federal portion of the tax is refundable to non-residents on non-consumable items over $100 in value.

Federal tax (G.S.T.) refunds for visitors Goods and services tax refunds are available to international visitors on goods (not food, liquor or services) totaling $100 or more. Save all receipts. Details and forms are available throughout tourist shopping areas. You can also contact Revenue Canada Visitor Rebate Program, Ottawa, Canada K1A 1J5; or phone within Canada (800)-668-4748; outside Canada (613) 991-3346.

Store opening hours: In general, Greater Vancouver's stores, shops and malls are open daily from 9 or 9:30 a.m. to 6 p.m. Monday, Tuesday, Wednesday and Saturday. On Thursdays and Fridays most remain open until 9 p.m. Many, but not all stores are open on Sundays from 11 a.m. or 12 noon to 5 p.m. Independent shops set extended or reduced hours at will. Shops (not malls) in tourist areas open into the early evening in summer.

Stamps: Postage of all sorts is available in kiosks at the back of many pharmacies and convenience stores. Look for the red and white "Canada Post" label in the window. At the time of this writing, the nominal stamp rate for delivery inside Canada is 45¢; for the United States, 52¢; for international destinations, 90¢. G.S.T. is applied to these rates. There is no special postcard rate. For additional information, call Vancouver Canada Post Corp., (604) 662-5722.

Time Zones: Vancouver is on Pacific Standard time (PST) from late October through March. During the summer, it is on Pacific Daylight time. The earth rotates in an eastward direction and PST is eight hours earlier than GMT (Greenwich Mean Time). For example: 12 noon in Vancouver is 8 p.m. in London.

Exact local time updates are available by dialing (604) 299-9000, extension 3322.

Lonely for **American news**? Phone (604) 299-9000, extension 3123 or 3121. News is updated throughout the day.

Lonely for **international news**? Phone (604) 299-9000, extension 3121.

BC Highway road conditions: Phone (604) 299-9000 , extension 7623.

Restaurant menus are posted outside or are available for previewing before entering any Vancouver eating establishment.

Vancouver Basics

Emergency

Police or ambulance
911
For lesser emergencies, consult the phone numbers inside front cover of the telephone book
Vancouver City Police (604) 717-3535
Royal Canadian Mounted Police (604) 264-3111
US Customs (360)332-5771
Canada Citizenship and Immigration (604) 666-2171 or (604) 299-9000, extension 3487

Canada Customs and Revenue Agency G.S.T. (604) 689-5411
Foreign Consulates American (604) 685-4311
German (604) 684-8377
British (604)683-4421
Australian (604) 684-1177
Japanese (604) 684-5868
Public City Transportation BC Transit for city bus, Skytrain, Sea Bus (604) 521-0400 or (604) 299-9000, extension 2233
Public Ferry Crossings BC Ferry Corporation 1-888-223-3779 or (604) 299-9000, extension 7444
Long Distance Telephone Service: Dial 0 or consult the BC TEL white pages
Medical attention: Most hotels keep a list of on-call doctors. Otherwise, go to the nearest hospital emergency department. Consult the BC TEL white pages.
No appointment necessary medical clinics: Medical doctors take new patients. Consult the BC Tel white pages.
Open 9 a.m. to 9 p.m. weekdays or 10 a.m. to 6 p.m. weekends, the Maple Medical Clinic is at #103, 2025 West Broadway, (604) 730-9769.
All-night pharmacy, open 24 hours: Shoppers Drug Mart, 1125 Davie St., Vancouver, (604) 669-2424; Shoppers Drud Mart, 2302 W. 4th Ave. (604) 738-3138; Shoppers Drug Mart, 885 W. Broadway (604) 708-1135.
Several other pharmacies are open until midnight. Consult the BC TEL yellow pages.

Lost? Marine Airsearch, or Search and Rescue (800) 567-5111
Highway Road Conditions (604) 299-9000, extension 7623

Index

A

accommodations, 65, 66
antique shops, 74
aquarium, 30, 38
architectural walking tour, 32
art galleries, 21, 72-75
    Emily Carr Institute of Art & Design,   58
    The Inuit Gallery, 51
    Vancouver Art Gallery, 30, 38
art walk, 75
artists, 75
automobile insurance, 114
automobile rentals, 16

B

ballet, 80-81
banking, 114
bars, 82-87
basketball, 89, 90
beaches. See parks & beaches
beer, 109
beluga whales, 41
bicycling, 36, 91-92
bingo halls, 82
bird sanctuary, 102
bird-watching, 101, 102
boating, 15, 36, 38, 94
bridges, 31, 40, 63
Burnaby Lake, 100
bus tours, 47
    See also driving tours; walking
            tours

C

Canada Place, 65
canoeing, 94

car insurance, 114
car rentals, 16
casinos, 82
children's activities, 36-40
Chinatown, 51-57
cigars, 58
city views, 49, 67, 112
climate, 7, 10-11
coffee houses, 107
comedy clubs, 86
concerts, 76, 81
crafts, 35, 51, 74, 78
cruises, 15, 29
culture, 17-19, 71-103
currency exchange, 114
cycling, 36, 91-92

D

dancing. See performing arts
Dead Man's Island, 61
Deighton, Jack, 53
dining, 105-113
    See also native cuisine
driving tours
    Downtown, 43-45
    North Shore, 31, 45-48
    Public Gardens, 48-49

E

emergency numbers, 115
entertainment, 81-82
    See also specific type of
            entertainment
entertainment industry, 19
environment, 24-25

F
ferry information, 115
festivals, 20, 33, 37, 81, 85
fireworks, 32
fish hatchery, 31
fishing, 79, 103
flea market, 59
football, 90, 91
forest industry, 24, 35

G
gaming establishments, 82
gardens, 48-49, 68-69
   Bloedel Floral Conservatory &
Quarry Gardens, 27, 65
   U.B.C.Botanical Garden, 69, 102
   VanDusen Botanical Garden, 30,
69, 103
Gastown, 51-53
golf, 96-98
Goods & Services Tax (GST), 114, 115
Granville Island, 27, 55, 57-58
Grouse Mountain, 31

H
harbour cruises, 15, 29
helplines & reference
   information, 16, 114-115
hiking, 65, 98-103
history
   of the Arts, 71-72
   of Vancouver, 22-23
hockey, 89, 90
Holocaust Education Centre, 79
Hotel Vancouver, 66

I
IMAX theatres, 27, 29

J
jade, 35, 56
jogging, 92-94

K
kayaking, 94
kids' activities, 36-40
Krall, Diana, 84

L
laser tag, 40
library, 36, 80
limousine tours, 47

M
malls. See shopping
mansions, 31, 35
maps, 8-9, 64
   Granville Island, 55
   Stanley Park, 60
markets, 58-59
medical information, 115
metric/Imperial conversions, 114
micro-breweries, 109
mini-golf, 36, 40
money, Canadian, 114
Moore, Greg, 92
motor racing, 90, 92, 93
mountain biking, 91-92
movie show times, 40
   See also IMAX theatres
museums, 78-80
   B.C.Sports Hall of Fame &
      Museum, 40, 78, 93
   Canadian Craft Museum, 35, 78
   Jade World, 35
   Museum of the Exotic World, 35, 80
   North Shore Museum and
      Archives, 80

Roedde House Museum, 67, 80
Rogers Sugar Museum, 32, 79
Science World, 29
U.B.C.Museum of Anthropology, 30, 78
Vancouver Maritime Museum, 30, 38, 78
Vancouver Museum, 30, 78
Vancouver Police Centennial Museum, 35, 80
music, 80-82
   See also festivals; performers; performing arts

N
native art & culture, 20-21, 75
native cuisine, 21, 105
nature walks, 61, 99-103
   See also parks & beaches
neighbourhoods, 11-16
nightclubs & pubs, 82-87
North Shore, 31-32

O
observatory, 79
opera, 81

P
paintball, 40
parks & beaches
   Ambleside Beach Park, 63
   Capilano River Regional Park, 98
   Capilano Suspension Bridge and Park, 31, 98
   Garry Point Park, 100
   Grant Narrows Regional Park, 100
   Jericho Beach Park, 38, 101
   Kitsilano Beach Park, 63
   Lighthouse, 35, 99

Lynn Canyon Park, 40, 63
Maplewood Farm, 32
Musqueum Park, 102
Queen Elizabeth Park, 65
Richmond Nature Park, 102
Seyour Demonstration Forest, 99
Stanley Park, 29, 36, 59, 61-63, 99
performers, 19
   See also festivals; music; performing arts
performing arts, 75-78
   Kitsilano Showboat, 35
Pitch & Putt, 36, 40
planetarium, 27-28, 78
playgrounds, indoor, 37
population, 11
postal services, 114
provincial flower, 48
public transit, 16
pubs & nightclubs, 82-87

R
railway excursions, 46
rainforest trails, 63, 98-99
Rebagliati, Ross, 95
restaurants, 105-113
road conditions, 115
Robson Street, 49-51
rollerblade rentals, 36
rowing, 61
Royal Hudson Steam Train, 46
running, 92-94

S
salmon fishing industry, 25, 31
science centres, 29, 35
shipping, 16-17, 78
shopping, 58, 114
   Canadiana, 54, 57
   Gastown, 51

shopping *(continued)*
  Robson Street, 49-51
sightseeing excursion companies, 47
Sister Cities, 63
skiing, 96
snowboarding, 95
sports, 78, 88, 89-98
sports bars, 87
Stanley Park, 29, 36, 59, 61-63, 99
Stanley Park's Flower Garden, 69
steam train excursions, 46
stock exchange, 36
store hours, 114
suspension bridges, 31, 40, 63
swimming pools, 36, 37, 38, 39, 63
symphony, 81

T
teen activities, 39-40
theatres, 38, 75-78
Three Greenhorns, 50
totem poles, 62
tourist information facilities, 16, 65
tours
  architectural, 32
  excursion companies, 46, 47
  See also driving tours; walking
      tours
trade shows, 34
train excursions, 46
transit, public, 16
trees, 101
trolley tours, 47

U
U.B.C.Botanical Garden, 69, 102

V
Vancouver Tourism, 16

Vancouverites, 17-19
VanDusen Botanical Garden, 30,
  69, 103
vehicle entry & insurance, 114
vehicle rentals, 16
Victoria, 69
views of city, 67, 112

W
walking tours
  architectural, 32
  art, 75
  Downtown, 65-68
  Gastown & Chinatown, 51-57
  Granville Island, 57-58
  Public Gardens, 68-69
  Robson Street, 49-51
  Stanley Park, 61-63
  West Vancouver Centennial
      Seawall, 65
  See also hiking; parks & beaches
water sports, 94
water parks. See swimming pools
weather, 7, 10-11
Whistler, 68
wildlife, 25, 102

Y
yacht charters, 30

Z
zoos, 36, 38

Reference

About the Author

Pat Kramer writes special interest guides for travellers who yearn to discover western Canada. She writes not for the generic "tourists," but for travel connoisseurs who delight in well planned trips filled with hidden wonders that are often overlooked.

Because she is a part-time tour director, her books concentrate on visitors' best-loved attractions. The result of her research, interesting stories and colourful photographs is a pleasurable guide on Vancouver's highlights.

It will be difficult for you to read about all these places without wanting to get up and see them for yourself.

Among Kramer's other special interest guidebooks are: *Native Sites in Western Canada* and *Totem Poles,* (both of which have been translated into German), *Gardens of British Columbia,* and *B.C. for Free and Almost Free*. Pat maintains several Web pages using keywords from her book titles. E-mail is at these sites. Come visit.

Photography Credits

Al Harvey: 4-5, 6, 10, 11, 12, 14, 15, 26, 27, 28, 35, 39, 42, 43, 44, 45, 47, 48 top, 49, 50, 59, 76, 77, 86, 88, 89, 90, 93, 94, 96, 98, 101, 102

Joseph King: 7, 17, 18, 20, 30, 32, 36, 38, 40, 41, 46, 51, 52, 53, 56, 62, 63, 66, 67, 68, 69, 70, 71, 72, 74, 75, 78, 79, 80, 83, 85, 103, 104, 105, 110, 113

Douglas Leighton: Front cover, back cover

Ricardo Ordóñez: Left front cover inset

Dennis Schmidt: 48 bottom, 100